THE VEGETABLE DISHES I CAN'T LIVE WITHOUT

☀ Other Books ☀
by
Mollie Katzen

☀ ☀ ☀ ☀ ☀ ☀

Eat, Drink, and Weigh Less (with Walter Willett, M.D.)

Mollie Katzen's Sunlight Café

The Enchanted Broccoli Forest

Mollie Katzen's Vegetable Heaven

Still Life with Menu

Moosewood Cookbook

Pretend Soup (with Ann Henderson)

Honest Pretzels

Salad People

☀ ☀ ☀ ☀ ☀ ☀ ☀ ☀ ☀ ☀ ☀ ☀

THE VEGETABLE DISHES I CAN'T LIVE WITHOUT

RECIPES and DRAWINGS
by Mollie Katzen

HYPERION

NEW YORK

Library of Congress Cataloging-in-Publication Data
Katzen, Mollie
        The vegetable dishes I can't live without / Mollie Katzen.
                p. cm.
1. Cookery (Vegetables) 1. Title.
        ISBN: 978-1-4013-2232-8
        TX801.K3775 2007
        641.6'51 — dc22   2007018547

Hyperion books are available for special promotions, premiums, or corporate training. For details contact Michael Rentas, Proprietary Markets, Hyperion, 77 West 66th Street, 12th floor, New York, New York 10023, or call 212-456-0133.

10 9 8 7 6 5 4 3

For Judith Bazell (1949–1972)

CONTENTS

ACKNOWLEDGMENTS

Many thanks to Christine Swett, who has been working with me for more than a decade now as a recipe test partner and reality checkpoint on everything culinary. My daughter, Eve Shames, has a great palate and an appreciation for vegetables, both of which have kept me going in the kitchen in fresh and new ways. Thank you, Eve, for tasting and sharing. My mother, Betsy Katzen, sent me all her vegetable recipe clippings from women's magazines—plus 3 x 5 card versions of her and her friends' favorites (many of them centered on canned soup) dating back to about 1952. She also continued to share her great enthusiasm throughout this project, as always. Thanks to my father, Leon Katzen, as well, for your love—and for your example of a very long life beautifully lived. May we all follow in your footsteps! My son, Sam Black, has been a great inspiration to me, as I've had the privilege to witness his ever-deepening devotion to his art and its craft, with focus, dedication, passion, and fine, fine taste in all things, food included. Much appreciation to Beth Shepard and Marissa Moss for daily reality checks and enthusiasm.

Untold thanks to my fabulous support team at Hyperion: Bob Miller, Ellen Archer, Will Schwalbe, Navorn Johnson, Fritz Metsch, Chisomo Kalinga, Claire McKean, Allison McGeehon, Michelle Ishay, Anna Campbell, Jessica Wiener, Jane Comins, Anton Markous, and Tina Bliss. You have been a pleasure to work with—flexible, generous, creative, patient, respectful, solution-oriented. My gratitude goes out in spades to each of you.

Robert MacKimmie has been a full-spectrum fellow traveler throughout this entire process. From the lush garden beds he designed to the beehives he installed in the rosemary patch to the lovingly tended fruit trees and worm bins to the wine, beer, and kombucha brewing—plus his exquisite photographic journaling of it all—Robert has helped me create a mini-agricultural paradise here at my home on the outskirts of Berkeley. My lifelong infatuation with green growing things and the systems that sustain them has thus been heightened and renewed exponentially. For this, and for Robert's support for all my work, I am deeply grateful.

THE VEGETABLE DISHES
I CAN'T LIVE WITHOUT

I love vegetables. Not just some of them sometimes, but most of them most of the time. Call me a leaf geek if you must. (And as you read these recipes, you'll probably call me a stem geek as well, which I'll happily accept.) I simply want to spread my enthusiasm through recipes, rather than through telling you You Should, as so many magazines and medical studies do these days. Okay, you should, but hopefully, also You Will Because You Want To—because vegetables are beautiful and accessible, and can be utterly and irresistibly tasty.

Is this a vegetarian book? Sure, if you define vegetarian as being pro-vegetable.

Are meat eaters allowed to use these recipes? Absolutely! The fact is, there's room on *all* of our plates for more vegetables, and we have much to discover along the way. And most of us, no matter how earnest and well meaning, don't eat quite enough vegetables. This could be due to any number of perceived limitations: time, interest, energy, refrigerator space, imagination. Also, we tend to assume that vegetables are dreary, and we often can't think of what to do with them past the salad course, if we even get that far. Here, then, just for you: a book of happy ideas for Beyond Salad, and then some!

It is easy to make vegetables taste wonderful through simple preparations utilizing a very few choice ingredients (including specific uses of heat, which in and of themselves are seasonings): extra-virgin olive oil, fresh garlic, roasted nut oil, tiny touches of salt and pepper, an herb or two, a very hot oven or a sizzling pan—or a very slow oven and a simmering pan. The willingness to focus on a few details for a few minutes here and there is key, and the vegetables themselves will shine, with everything falling deliciously into place.

These are my current ninety-something favorite vegetable recipes. "Current," because this list shifts around with the seasons, and the inherent moods—and produce—they deliver. I hope you will try a broad range of these mostly simple dishes, and then possibly even be inspired to prepare several at a time and serve them together, showcasing contrasting colors, textures, and flavors. If you add even one new vegetable dish a week to your repertoire, you will be rewarded in many ways. I promise.

Mollie Katzen

Artichoke Heart & Spinach
GRATIN

Layers of artichoke hearts and spinach—with a crunchy topping of bread crumbs and cheese.

NOTES:

♥ Make your own coarse bread crumbs by drying out some of your favorite bread, and then crumbling it either by hand (in a plastic bag, so it won't go all over the place) or in a food processor with the steel blade (a few spurts).

♥ This dish keeps for several days, covered and refrigerated—and reheats (in an oven, toaster oven, or microwave) very well.

> 1 12-ounce bag frozen artichoke hearts
> 1 pound fresh baby spinach leaves (or 1 pound frozen chopped spinach)
> 1 tablespoon extra-virgin olive oil
> 1 cup finely minced onion
> 2 teaspoons minced or crushed garlic
> ¼ teaspoon salt
> Freshly ground black pepper, to taste
> ½ cup coarse bread crumbs
> ⅓ cup grated Parmesan cheese

1) Preheat the oven to 375°F.

2) Place the artichoke hearts in a colander and run under tap water to defrost. Set aside to drain thoroughly.

3) Place the spinach in a separate colander and rinse well. Shake to remove most, but not all, of the water clinging to the leaves. (If using frozen spinach, thaw it in a colander under running tap water and then let it drain well—pressing out most of the excess liquid with the back of a spoon. It doesn't have to be bone-dry—just not soupy.)

4) Place a large, deep skillet (with an ovenproof handle) over medium heat. After about a minute, add the olive oil and swirl to coat the pan. Add the onion and sauté for about 5 minutes, or until translucent.

5) Increase the heat to medium-high, add the spinach, and cover. Cook, tossing occasionally, for 3 to 4 minutes, or until wilted. Remove the cover and continue to cook, tossing occasionally, for about 10 minutes, or until the liquid released by the spinach mostly evaporates.

6) Turn the heat back down to medium, then add the garlic, salt, and a few grinds of black pepper. Sauté until the garlic is fragrant (2 to 3 minutes), then stir in the drained artichoke hearts and remove from the heat.

7) Smooth the top surface with the back of a spoon, and sprinkle the bread crumbs evenly over the top, followed by an even layer of cheese.

8) Bake, uncovered, for 10 to 15 minutes, or until the Parmesan is golden and the bread crumbs have turned golden and crispy. Serve hot or warm.

~ Yield: 6 servings ~

Grilled Lemon-Spiked Artichokes

When you stuff a precooked split artichoke with a chunk of fresh lemon and flash-sauté the whole arrangement in hot olive oil, the result is stunning, both visually and flavorwise.

NOTES:
- ♥ Meyer lemons add a terrific, perfumed flavor—and are well worth the price (if you don't live in California and pick them from your own tree). But you can use standard grocery store lemons as well.
- ♥ The artichokes get cooked twice: steamed until tender, and then quickly sautéed with the lemon. The first steaming can be done up to several days ahead of time.

        2 large artichokes
        1 large lemon or 2 smaller ones
        1 to 2 tablespoons extra-virgin olive oil

1) Use a sharp knife to slice off the top inch or so of each artichoke and trim the tough tip from the stem. Use scissors to snip off the sharp leaf tips.

2) Cook the artichokes in a vegetable steamer over simmering water until a knife can easily be inserted into the base of each one. Remove them with tongs and place them upside down in a colander in the sink to drain.

3) When the artichokes are thoroughly drained, cut them in half lengthwise with a sharp knife, then use a small spoon to scrape out the fuzzy choke. The artichokes can be prepared up to this point and stored, in an airtight container at room temperature, for several hours—or in the refrigerator for several days.

4) Cut the lemons into quarters (or halves if using smaller ones). Tuck a piece of lemon into the cavity of each artichoke so that the flat, cut surface of the lemon is flush with the flat, cut surface of the artichoke, and the lemon's peel is nestled against the inside of the artichoke.

5) Shortly before serving time, place a medium-sized skillet over medium heat. After about a minute, add the olive oil and swirl to coat the pan. Place the artichokes, lemon-side down, in the hot oil, and let them cook undisturbed for about 2 minutes, or until the lemon is golden. Flip the artichokes over and continue cooking another 2 minutes, lemon-side up. Serve hot, warm, or at room temperature.

~ Yield: 4 servings (half an artichoke each) ~

Arugula~Pecan Pesto

Grinding flavorful green leaves into a delicious paste provides a great opportunity for packing a full serving of vegetables into a few exquisite bites. This arugula version is truly revelatory! The peppery, slightly bitter flavor is enriched by the pecans and softened by the light, sweet (and hardly discernible) presence of golden raisins.

NOTES:
- The pecans do not need to be toasted, but you can experiment with toasting them lightly to see if you prefer the slightly enhanced flavor.
- The pesto will keep for up to a week in a tightly covered container in the refrigerator. A thin layer of olive oil over the top surface will help preserve it.

> 4 packed cups arugula (about 8 ounces)
> 1 small clove garlic
> 1 cup chopped pecans (toasting optional)
> 1/4 teaspoon salt (or more)
> 1 to 2 teaspoons lemon juice (or to taste)
> 1 to 2 tablespoons (packed measure) golden raisins (or more)
> 5 to 6 tablespoons extra-virgin olive oil (possibly more)

1) Place the arugula, garlic, pecans, and salt in a food processor fitted with the steel blade. Pulse until pulverized, adding the lemon juice and raisins as you go.

2) Run the processor again, drizzling in the olive oil in a steady stream. When it reaches the consistency that looks right to you, stop the machine. Transfer the pesto to a small container with a tight-fitting lid. Taste to adjust the lemon juice and salt.

3) Smooth the top of the pesto with the back of a spoon, and add a thin layer of olive oil to cover the top. Cover and chill. Serve as desired.

~ Yield: 1 1/3 cups ~

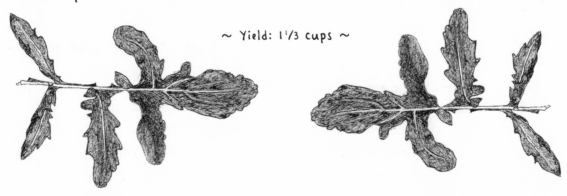

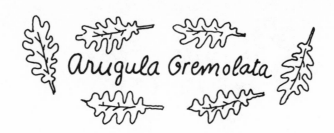

Arugula Gremolata

Traditional gremolata is a feathery mix of finely rendered parsley, garlic, and lemon zest—most notably used as a topping for the Italian dish osso buco. This feisty spin-off (made in seconds in a food processor) replaces the parsley with arugula, and offers the option of orange zest in place of lemon.

NOTES:

♥ Young, small (and therefore not-so-bitter) arugula is best for this. Just pinch off any stem extending past the base of the leaf and use the rest. With older, larger arugula, remove and use only the leaves, and discard the stems.

♥ This recipe is very easily multiplied or divided to make exactly the amount you need.

♥ Make it and use it—it doesn't improve with age.

♥ Zesting the lemon peel (with a zester or a good vegetable peeler) and then mincing it very finely with a sharp knife is preferable to grating the zest, which could make it a bit bitter.

♥ I like to serve this on pasta (especially the farfalle, or bow-tie, shape), as in the augmented recipe that follows.

> 2 cups (loosely packed) young arugula (or older arugula without stems), about 2 ounces
> 4 teaspoons finely minced garlic
> 4 teaspoons finely minced lemon or orange zest
> Salt and freshly ground black pepper, to taste

1) Combine the arugula, garlic, and lemon zest in the bowl of a food processor.

2) Pulse to finely chop—don't purée! Season to taste with the salt and pepper. That's it—it's now ready to use.

~ Yield: ¾ cup (enough for 4 pasta servings) ~

 # FARFALLE

with
Arugula Gremolata,
Gorgonzola,
Golden Raisins,
& Walnuts

3/4 pound farfalle (bow-tie pasta)
2 to 3 tablespoons extra-virgin olive oil
1 recipe Arugula Gremolata (preceding recipe)
½ cup (heaping measure) crumbled gorgonzola
2 to 3 tablespoons golden raisins
1 cup very small, very sweet cherry tomatoes (optional)
½ cup minced walnuts, lightly toasted
Freshly ground black pepper, to taste

1) Cook the pasta in plenty of boiling water until al dente. Drain and transfer to a serving bowl. Immediately toss with the olive oil.

2) Add the remaining ingredients, except the walnuts and pepper. Toss until thoroughly combined.

3) Serve immediately, topped with the walnuts and a generous application of black pepper.

~ Yield: 4 servings ~

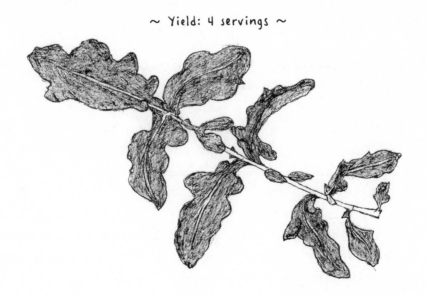

Asparagus Crêpes
with Mushroom Sauce

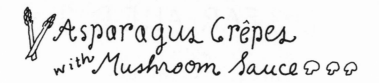

NOTE:

♥ You can make the crêpes—and cook the asparagus—up to several days ahead of time. Leave the pancakes stacked on the plate, then wrap the whole thing tightly in plastic wrap and refrigerate until you're ready to fill them and serve. Refrigerate the cooked asparagus in a sealed plastic bag.

> 1 large egg
> 1¼ cups milk
> 1 cup unbleached all-purpose flour
> ¼ teaspoon salt
> A little melted butter for the pan
> 1½ pounds asparagus (average thickness), trimmed
>   and steamed until tender
> Mushroom Sauce (recipe follows)

1) Place the egg, milk, flour, and salt in a blender and whip until smooth.

2) Heat a 6- or 7-inch nonstick crêpe or omelet pan. When it is warm, brush it lightly with melted butter. Wait another 30 seconds or so until the pan is quite hot.

3) When the pan is hot enough to sizzle a bread crumb, pour in ¼ cup of the batter. Lift the pan, and tilt it in all directions until the batter thoroughly coats the bottom. Pour off any excess batter. (The pancake should be thin.)

4) Cook on one side until set (about 20 seconds), then turn it over and cook for just another second or two on the other side.

5) Turn the crêpe out onto a clean, dry dinner plate and repeat the procedure until you have used up all the batter. (If you keep the pan hot, you won't need to add much—if any—additional butter.) You can pile the finished crêpes on the plate; they won't stick together.

6) To fill, place 3 or 4 stalks of cooked asparagus on one side of each crêpe, and roll or fold the other side over. Serve warm or at room temperature, with hot or warm Mushroom Sauce puddled onto the plate underneath and/or spooned over the top.

~ Yield: 4 to 5 servings (about 2 crêpes apiece) ~

MUSHROOM SAUCE

NOTE:

♥ It's easiest to warm the milk directly in a measuring cup in a microwave oven.

3 tablespoons unsalted butter
1 pound mushrooms, thinly sliced
6 medium-sized shiitake mushrooms, stemmed and thinly sliced
  (optional)
½ teaspoon salt (possibly more, to taste)
3 tablespoons brandy or dry sherry
3 tablespoons unbleached all-purpose flour
1½ cups warmed milk
Freshly ground black pepper

1) Melt the butter in a medium-sized skillet. Add all the mushrooms and the salt, and cook over medium heat for about 10 minutes, stirring occasionally.

2) Add the brandy or sherry, and cook for 5 minutes more.

3) Gradually sprinkle in the flour as you whisk the mushroom mixture. Whisk and cook for another 5 minutes over medium heat.

4) Stir in the warmed milk. Cook over low heat, stirring often, until thickened and smooth (about 5 more minutes). Season to taste with black pepper and additional salt, if desired. Serve hot.

~ Yield: About 2½ cups ~

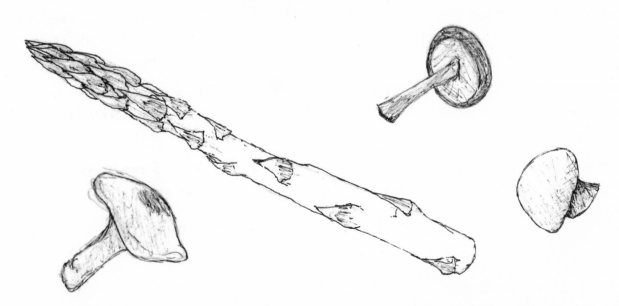

Gingered Asparagus

Flavoring vinegar with ginger creates major kitchen incense! This is a wonderful way to enjoy asparagus as either a salad or a side dish. (The definitions happily blur.)

NOTES:
- ♥ You can prepare the vinegar (step 1) well ahead of time. It can sit, covered, up to 2 days at room temperature, and will only get better. Meanwhile, the asparagus can marinate deeply in the garlic-spiked oil (step 3).
- ♥ Assemble the finished dish at the last minute, so the acid from the vinegar won't discolor the asparagus.

> ¾ cup cider vinegar or unseasoned rice vinegar
> 1½ tablespoons minced fresh ginger
> 2 tablespoons light-colored honey
> 1 pound fresh asparagus, tough ends trimmed
> ½ teaspoon minced or crushed garlic
> 2 tablespoons Chinese-style dark sesame oil
> 3 tablespoons canola oil or peanut oil
> ¼ teaspoon salt (possibly more, to taste)
> 1 teaspoon soy sauce

1) Place the vinegar and ginger in a small saucepan and bring to a boil. Turn the heat to medium-low, and cook, uncovered, for 10 to 15 minutes, or until the vinegar is reduced by about half. (Open the windows!) Remove from the heat and stir in the honey. Set aside.

2) Steam the asparagus until just tender (not too soft). Refresh under cold running water immediately and drain well. Dry thoroughly with paper towels and transfer to a platter or a plate with a rim, arranging the asparagus in a single layer.

3) Whisk together the garlic, oils, salt, and soy sauce in a small bowl. Pour this mixture over the asparagus, then cover tightly with plastic wrap and refrigerate for at least 2 hours and up to 2 days.

4) Shortly before serving, spoon the vinegar mixture over the asparagus, distributing it as evenly as possible. (Definitely include all those little bits of ginger!) Serve chilled or at room temperature.

~ Yield: 4 to 5 servings ~

Roasted Asparagus
WITH
Pomegranate~Lime Glaze

NOTES:

♥ You can roast asparagus of any thickness. Simply keep your eye on it, and take it out of the oven just before it is completely tender. (It will continue to cook from its own heat for another few minutes, and you don't want it too soft.)

♥ Pomegranate molasses is a thick, delicious reduction of pure pomegranate juice, available at Middle Eastern food shops or in the imported foods section of many grocery stores. It will keep forever in your cupboard.

> 1 tablespoon extra-virgin olive oil (possibly more)
> 1 pound asparagus, tough ends trimmed or snapped off
> ¼ cup pomegranate molasses
> 1 tablespoon plus 1 teaspoon fresh lime juice
> Salt, to taste

1) Preheat the oven to 425°F. Line a baking sheet with foil and brush or spread it generously with oil.

2) Distribute the asparagus on the prepared baking sheet and roll them around so they will be completely coated with oil.

3) Place the baking sheet on the center rack of the oven and roast for about 3 minutes. Shake the baking sheet and/or use tongs to reposition the asparagus so it can roast evenly all over.

4) Meanwhile, combine the pomegranate molasses and lime juice in a small bowl and whisk until smooth. Set aside.

5) Back to the asparagus: After another couple of minutes in the oven, begin checking for doneness. Remove from the oven as soon as the asparagus is "this side of tender." You can salt it lightly, if you wish. Serve hot, warm, or at room temperature, with room-temperature glaze puddled underneath or drizzled on top (or both).

~ Yield: 3 to 4 servings ~

Tarragon~Pecan Asparagus

Really good—and best when served within an hour of being made.

> 1½ pounds asparagus
> 2 tablespoons balsamic vinegar or cider vinegar
> 2 teaspoons light-colored honey
> 2 tablespoons extra-virgin olive oil
> 1 cup minced pecans, lightly toasted
> Up to 1 tablespoon minced or crushed garlic
> ½ teaspoon salt (or to taste)
> 1 to 2 tablespoons minced fresh tarragon (or 2 teaspoons dried)
> Freshly ground black pepper, to taste

1) Break off and discard the tough bottom ends of the asparagus, then slice the stalks on the diagonal into 1½-inch pieces. Set aside.

2) Combine the vinegar and honey in a small bowl and mix until the honey dissolves. Set aside.

3) Place a large, deep skillet over medium heat. After about a minute, add the olive oil and swirl to coat the pan. Add the pecans and sauté over medium-low heat for about 10 minutes, or until they are fragrant and lightly toasted.

4) Turn the heat to medium-high, and add the asparagus, garlic, and salt. Stir-fry for about 3 to 5 minutes, or until the asparagus is just barely tender. (Thicker asparagus will take longer.)

5) Add the vinegar mixture to the asparagus, stirring well. Cook over high heat for only about 30 seconds longer, then remove from the heat.

6) Stir in the tarragon, more salt if you like, and some black pepper to taste. Serve hot, warm, or at room temperature.

~ Yield: 4 to 5 servings ~

Avocado ❤ Strawberry Saladita

"Saladita" is my term for a colorful, slightly unusual medley of diced vegetables (and often fruit) that is served cold or at room temperature as a side dish, relish, topping — anywhere you would use a salsa. This one is really stunning — delicious on or next to grilled tofu, chicken, or fish, it is also a great little appetizer on its own.

NOTE:
❤ This doesn't keep well, so plan on serving it soon after it is assembled.

> 3 to 4 tablespoons fresh lime juice
> 1 cup diced strawberries (sweet, flavorful ones!)
> 3 to 4 tablespoons minced crystallized ginger
> ½ cup peeled, diced jicama
> 1 medium firm-but-ripe avocado, in tiny dice
> Salt, to taste (optional)

1) In a medium-large bowl, combine all the ingredients except the avocado and salt, and mix well.

2) Gently stir in the avocado dice (plus a dash of salt, if you like) and serve soon.

~ Yield: About 6 servings ~

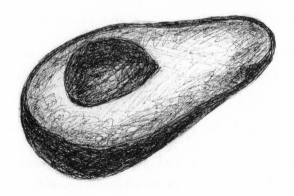

Beet-Avocado-Pear "Carpaccio"

Thin slices of beautifully contrasting ingredients are arranged in shallow layers on a plate and sprinkled with touches of extra flavor, texture, and color. Serve this as an elegant first course for dinner, or as a main dish for lunch.

NOTES:
- ♥ You can cook the beets any way you prefer—by steaming, boiling, or roasting. (Roasting instructions are on the opposite page.)
- ♥ Cut the pear and avocado just before using, so they won't turn brown.

A few handfuls of very fresh arugula leaves
1 pound beets, cooked until tender, then peeled and thinly sliced
1 to 2 tablespoons roasted walnut oil or extra-virgin olive oil
1 medium firm-but-ripe avocado
1 tablespoon cider vinegar
Salt, to taste (optional)
2 medium-sized perfectly ripe pears, in thin slices (peeling optional)
1 tablespoon fresh lemon juice
¼ cup crumbled Roquefort or Gorgonzola cheese
½ cup minced walnuts, lightly toasted

OPTIONAL GARNISHES:
- ♥ Pomegranate seeds
- ♥ Dried cranberries (or minced fresh cranberries)
- ♥ Squeezable lemon wedges
- ♥ Freshly ground black pepper, to taste

1) Scatter the arugula onto a medium-large serving platter, or on 4 or 5 individual plates.

2) Place the beet slices over the arugula. Drizzle the beets with oil.

3) Halve the avocado, then pit, peel, and cut it into long thin slices. Arrange these around the beets and immediately drizzle the avocado surfaces with vinegar to keep them from discoloring. Sprinkle very lightly with salt, if you desire.

4) Lay the pear slices on or around the avocado, then sprinkle everything with lemon juice.

5) Toss the crumbled cheese over the top and garnish with walnuts, pomegranate seeds, or cranberries, and a wedge of lemon. Serve immediately, passing around the pepper mill.

~ Yield: 4 to 5 servings ~

Roasted Beets
WITH
Tart Pink Grapefruit Glaze

Major color—especially if you use an assortment of beets! This a delicious way to spark them with a big hit of zingy flavor.

NOTES:
- ♥ Make the glaze when the beets come out of the oven. It only takes about 10 minutes.
- ♥ A high-grade maple syrup (one with very subtle flavor) works best for this.

> 3 pounds beets
> 1 cup fresh-squeezed pink grapefruit juice
> 1 tablespoon unseasoned rice vinegar
> 2 tablespoons plus 2 teaspoons real maple syrup
> 1 tablespoon cornstarch

1) Preheat the oven to 450°F.

2) Trim the greens from the beets, leaving on about 1 inch of the stems. Divide the beets into 2 groups, wrapping each in a bundle of foil, with about 3 tablespoons of water tossed in. Roast in the center of the oven for up to 1 hour, or until the beets are tender enough to be pierced with a fork. Remove the tray from the oven, open the foil packets, and let the beets cool on the tray until comfortable to handle. Then remove and discard the stems and rub off the skins. Cut the beets into thin slices.

3) In a medium-small bowl, whisk together the grapefruit juice, vinegar, and maple syrup.

4) Place the cornstarch in a small saucepan and drizzle in the grapefruit mixture, whisking until all the cornstarch is dissolved.

5) Place the pan over medium heat, and heat just to the boiling point, whisking frequently. Turn the heat down and cook, stirring often, for about 3 to 5 minutes, or until thickened and glossy. Remove from the heat.

6) Drizzle the hot glaze over the hot, warm, or room-temperature roasted beets, and serve right away.

~ Yield: 4 to 5 servings ~

✐ COMPLETE BEETS ✐

It seems like an obvious idea to serve beets together with their greens, but somehow I have always approached the opposite ends of the beet as two separate vegetables—until now. These days, my favorite thing to do with beets is to first cook the roots and leaves separately (and each according to its individual nature) and then to reunite them in one humble but outstanding dish.

NOTES:
- ♥ Beets and their greens don't always match. Sometimes you can find a bunch with perfect greens and roots, but other times, you need to mix and match. That's why the ingredient list is written as it is. When separating beets from their greens, give about 1 inch of the stem to the beets, and leave the rest of the stem with the greens. (Taking that "Complete" part literally, keep in mind that beet stems are edible.)
- ♥ You can cook the beets any way you prefer—by steaming, boiling, or roasting. (Roasting instructions are on the previous page.)

> 1½ pounds beets, cooked until tender
> 2 to 3 bunches beet greens, very fresh (about the volume of 2 small heads of leaf lettuce), with stems
> 2 tablespoons extra-virgin olive oil
> 1½ teaspoons minced or crushed garlic
> Salt, to taste
> 2 teaspoons cider vinegar (possibly more, to taste)

1) Peel the beets and cut them first into quarters, then crosswise into slices. (The size and shape of the pieces is up to you.)

2) Trim or discard any wilted or otherwise nonperky parts of the stems, then clean the greens plus the remaining stems in cold water and spin dry. Coarsely chop the leaves and stems, and set aside.

3) Place a medium-sized skillet over medium heat. After about a minute, add 1 teaspoon of the olive oil and swirl to coat the pan. Add ¼ teaspoon of the garlic, then immediately toss in the beets and stir-fry very quickly (less than a minute), just to get everything coated. Transfer to a medium-sized bowl, sprinkle with a little salt, and mix in the vinegar. Set aside.

4) Return the pan to the heat and swirl in the remaining olive oil. Add the beet greens and stems, turn up the heat to medium-high, and cook, lifting with tongs and moving the greens around for about a minute, or until they are just wilted but still brightly colored. Sprinkle with a little salt and add the remaining garlic. Cook and toss for about 3 minutes longer, or until wilted.

5) Add the beets back in, mixing thoroughly, then transfer everything back to the bowl. Taste to adjust the salt and to see if it might need a few additional drops of vinegar. Serve hot, warm, or at room temperature.

~ Yield: 4 to 5 servings ~

Bok Choy,
Broccoli Rabe,
& Shiitake Mushrooms
with Roasted Garlic

NOTE:

♥ Garlic appears twice in this recipe—in two forms, roasted and fresh—virtually as two different ingredients. The roasted garlic needs to be made at least 45 minutes to an hour ahead of time. You can get everything else cut and ready while the garlic roasts.

        2 tablespoons canola oil or peanut oil
        1 medium-sized garlic bulb
        1 small head bok choy (up to a pound)
        Half a medium bunch broccoli rabe (about ½ pound)
        1½ cups chopped onion
        10 medium-sized shiitake mushrooms, stemmed and quartered
        ¼ teaspoon salt (or to taste)
        1 teaspoon minced or crushed garlic
        Freshly ground black pepper, to taste

        OPTIONAL TOPPINGS:
        ♥ Roasted whole cashews
        ♥ Chinese-style dark sesame oil
        ♥ Chili oil

1) Preheat the oven or a toaster oven to 375°F. Line a small baking pan with foil and drizzle with a little of the oil. Trim the tips of the garlic, then stand the bulb upright on the oiled foil. Roast for 30 to 40 minutes, or until the bulb feels soft when gently squeezed. Remove from the oven and let cool. When comfortable to handle, break the bulb into individual cloves and squeeze the pulp from the skins. This will be a slightly sticky process and the bulbs may break apart a little—all of which is fine.

2) While the garlic roasts, prepare the bok choy and broccoli rabe. For the bok choy, trim and discard the tough bottom ¼ inch or so, if necessary. Remove and coarsely chop the leaves, and cut the stems into 1-inch pieces. Keep the leaves and stems separate. Trim the tough ends from the broccoli rabe and chop the rest into 1-inch pieces.

3) Place a large, deep skillet or wok over medium heat. After about a minute, add the remaining oil and swirl to coat the pan. Turn the heat to high, add the onion and shiitakes, and cook, stirring often, for about 2 minutes, or until the vegetables begin to brown. Add the bok choy stems and the broccoli rabe, sprinkling in the salt. Stir-fry for about 2 minutes, or until the stems are just tender. Toss in the bok choy leaves and about 1½ tablespoons water, then immediately cover the pan. Turn the heat down to medium and cook for about 2 more minutes (lifting the cover to stir just once or twice) until the stems are tender and the leaves wilted.

4) Add both the fresh and roasted garlic, tossing gently. Cook and stir for just a minute longer, until the garlic is fragrant. Season lightly with freshly ground black pepper, and serve immediately, topped with roasted whole cashews, if desired. Pass shaker bottles of Chinese-style dark sesame oil and chili oil for a finishing touch.

~ Yield: 4 servings ~

Bell Pepper Festival

Pile this colorful combination of soft sweet onions and crisp, bright, barely cooked peppers on top of (or in the case of rice or pasta, mixed in with) anything you want to spruce up: grilled tofu or fish, an open-faced cheese sandwich, an omelet, pasta, rice—really anything.

NOTE:
♥ This dish will keep for up to a week if stored in a tightly covered container in the refrigerator. You can then use it incrementally as desired.

> 2 tablespoons olive oil
> 1 cup thinly sliced onion
> 4 medium bell peppers (about 1½ pounds of assorted bright colors), thinly sliced
> ¼ teaspoon salt (or to taste)
> 1½ teaspoons minced or crushed garlic

1) Place a large, wide, shallow skillet over medium heat. After about a minute, add the olive oil and swirl to coat the pan.

2) Turn the heat to high and add the onion. Cook it quickly until it wilts and becomes translucent. This will take only about 3 to 5 minutes.

3) When the onion becomes very soft, add the peppers, salt, and garlic. After about a minute over strong heat, turn the heat down to medium, and continue to cook and stir (tongs work best!) for only about 5 minutes longer. The peppers should be barely cooked. Serve hot, warm, or at room temperature in any context.

~ Yield: 6 or more servings ~

Broccoli
dipped in
Wonderful Peanut Sauce

Children love this dish! The broccoli can be cooked up to several days ahead of time. Serve it at any temperature with room-temperature or warm sauce.

1 large bunch broccoli (1½ pounds)
1 cup good peanut butter (smooth, not chunky)
3 to 4 tablespoons light-colored honey
1 cup hot water
2 to 3 tablespoons soy or tamari sauce
1½ teaspoons minced or crushed garlic
2 teaspoons cider vinegar
3 to 4 tablespoons finely minced cilantro
Salt, to taste
Cayenne, to taste

1) Bring a large pot of water to a boil. In the meantime, trim and discard the tough stem end of the broccoli, and slice the rest lengthwise into about 6 to 8 hefty spears.

2) When the water boils, lower the heat to a simmer, and plunge in the broccoli for 2 minutes if you like it tender-crisp, and for 3 minutes if you like it tender-tender.

3) Drain in a colander, then put the broccoli under cold running water to cool it down. Drain thoroughly, then dry the broccoli by first shaking it emphatically and then by patting it with paper towels. Transfer to a zip-style plastic bag, seal it, and store until use.

4) Place the peanut butter and honey in a bowl. Add the hot water, and mash and stir patiently with a spoon or a small whisk until uniformly blended.

5) Stir in the remaining ingredients, adding salt and cayenne to taste, and mix well. Serve right away, surrounded by steamed broccoli of any temperature. (You can also cover it tightly and refrigerate for up to a week. Let the sauce come to room temperature before serving.)

~ Yield: 4 to 5 servings ~

BROCCOLI
 with Garlic,
Dried Tomatoes,
and Lemon

NOTES:
- ♥ First you blanch large pieces of broccoli in boiling water, after which you can store it for up to 5 days in the refrigerator. (Added benefit: It lasts longer after this cooking process and takes up less refrigerator space than when raw.) Then, just before serving, you give it a delicious warm-up in gently heated garlic-tomato-lemon infused olive oil for a perfect finish.
- ♥ For the most aesthetic results, use a zester to make lovely, long strands of lemon zest. (Grating is not recommended here.)

> 1 large bunch broccoli (1½ pounds)
> 3 ounces dried tomatoes (cut in half, or into smaller pieces, with scissors)
> 2 to 3 tablespoons extra-virgin olive oil
> 1 teaspoon minced or crushed garlic
> 1 tablespoon lemon zest (long strands, if possible)
> Salt, to taste
> Freshly ground black pepper, to taste
> Red pepper flakes (optional)

1) Bring a large pot of water to a boil. In the meantime, trim and discard the tough stem end of the broccoli and slice the rest lengthwise into about 6 to 8 hefty spears.

2) When the water boils, lower the heat to a simmer, and plunge in the broccoli for 2 minutes if you like it tender-crisp, and for 3 minutes if you like it tender-tender. Meanwhile, place the dried tomatoes in a large colander in the sink.

3) Pour the broccoli and all its water into the colander (soaking the tomatoes), and then refresh under cold running water. Drain thoroughly, then dry the broccoli and tomatoes first by shaking the colander, and then by patting everything with paper towels. Transfer to a zip-style plastic bag, seal it, and store until use. Bring to room temperature before finishing and serving.

4) About 15 minutes before serving time, place a large skillet over medium-low heat and add the olive oil. While you are waiting for it to heat, cut the broccoli into smaller pieces (whatever size and shape you prefer).

5) When the oil warms (after about 3 minutes), add the garlic and the broccoli-and-tomatoes mixture, turning the vegetables with tongs every few minutes. Continue doing this for 5 to 8 minutes (possibly even a little longer), until the broccoli and tomatoes are heated through, cooked to your liking, and delightfully coated with the garlic and oil. Toss in the lemon zest during the last minute or so of cooking, and continue to turn with tongs.

6) Add salt and pepper to taste, plus a sprinkling of red pepper flakes if you like, and serve hot or warm.

~ Yield: 4 servings ~

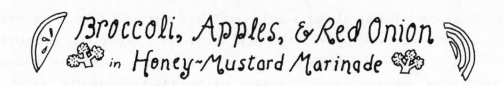

Broccoli, Apples, & Red Onion
in Honey-Mustard Marinade

Lightly cooked broccoli absorbs this tangy dressing beautifully. The sweet onions and tart green apple provide color and flavor contrasts. This can be made up to two days ahead of time if tightly covered and refrigerated. The broccoli will lose some of its color, but not its crunch.

NOTES:
- ♥ If you are not going to serve this right away, you might want to leave out the apple slices and add them shortly before serving.
- ♥ You can save the broccoli stems for making Broccoli Stem Pickles (opposite page).

1 large bunch broccoli (1½ pounds)	2 teaspoons light-colored honey
2 tablespoons cider vinegar	5 tablespoons extra-virgin olive oil
2 tablespoons Dijon mustard	¾ cup thinly sliced red onion
½ teaspoon minced or crushed garlic	1 medium-sized tart apple, thinly sliced
¼ teaspoon salt	Freshly ground black pepper, to taste

1) Put up a large saucepan of water to boil. While waiting for this to happen, remove and discard the thick lower stems of the broccoli, and cut the thinner upper stems and tops into medium-sized spears.

2) Measure the vinegar into a medium-large bowl. Use a small whisk to stir constantly as you add the mustard, garlic, salt, and honey.

3) Keep whisking as you drizzle in the oil in a steady stream. The mixture will thicken as the oil becomes incorporated.

4) By now the water should be boiling. Turn it down to a simmer and add the broccoli. Let it cook in the water for 1 to 2 minutes, or until it becomes very bright green and tender-crisp (to your liking). Meanwhile, place the sliced red onion in a large colander in the sink.

5) Pour the broccoli and all its water over the onion in the colander. (The hot water will wilt the onion slightly upon contact.) Place the colander of vegetables under cold running water for a few minutes, then shake to drain well.

6) Transfer the vegetables to the bowlful of dressing. Use tongs to toss until the broccoli is well coated, adding the apple slices as you go. You can serve this right away, or cover and let it marinate in the refrigerator, where the flavor will deepen. Serve cold or at room temperature, topped with freshly ground black pepper to taste.

~ Yield: 4 to 5 servings ~

Broccoli Stem Pickles

Those broccoli stalks that you normally might feel somewhat guilty discarding in favor of the lovelier crowns now have a destination: namely, the pickle jar! People love this unusual dish, and it's a great backdoor access to increased vegetable consumption.

NOTES:
- ♥ This recipe needs a minimum 4-hour pickling period, but a longer sit will make the pickles even better. They will stay good (crunchy, even!) for a good 2 weeks or longer.
- ♥ Seasoned rice vinegar, lightly salted and sweetened, is available in Asian grocery stores and in the imported foods section of good supermarkets.
- ♥ Be sure to choose broccoli with firm, crisp, intact stems for the best results.
- ♥ Use a sturdy vegetable peeler for peeling the stalks.

Stems from a large bunch of broccoli
  (at least 4 good, healthy stalks)
1 tablespoon light-colored honey
½ cup hot water
⅓ cup seasoned rice vinegar

1) Put up a large pot of water to boil.

2) In the meantime, remove and discard the tough bottom ends (about the last ¼ inch) of the stalks, then trim and peel the stalks. Cut them lengthwise about ⅛ inch thick, and then crosswise into matchsticks. You should have about 4 cups.

3) When the water boils, add the stems and lower the heat to a simmer. Cook for 1 to 2 minutes, until tender-crisp, and then drain into a colander in the sink. Refresh under cold running water for a minute or so, then drain again.

4) Place the honey in a medium-sized bowl and add the hot water. Stir until the honey dissolves, then add the vinegar and mix well.

5) Add the broccoli stems to the mixture, making sure they are completely submerged so they can "pickle." Let sit at room temperature for about 20 minutes, then transfer to a jar with a tight-fitting lid and refrigerate.

~ Yield: 4 to 5 servings ~

Sesame-Walnut-Ginger
❧ BROCCOLI ❧

A deeply flavored marinade, full of garlic and ginger, coats tender pieces of broccoli. Lightly toasted walnuts provide the crowning touch.

NOTE:
♥ This recipe needs a minimum 2-hour marinating period. You can also marinate it longer, which enables you to make the salad up to a day ahead of time.

> ⅓ cup roasted walnut oil
> 1 tablespoon Chinese-style dark sesame oil
> 1 tablespoon soy sauce
> 1 teaspoon salt
> 1 tablespoon finely minced fresh garlic
> 1 tablespoon finely minced fresh ginger
> Freshly ground black pepper, to taste
> Pinch of cayenne
> 2 pounds broccoli, cut into 2-inch spears
> ⅓ cup unseasoned rice vinegar
> 1½ cups walnut halves, lightly toasted

1) Combine the oils, soy sauce, salt, garlic, ginger, and black and cayenne peppers in a large bowl.

2) Steam the broccoli until just tender and bright green. Refresh under cold running water, then drain thoroughly and pat dry with paper towels. Add to the marinade and stir gently until well coated. Cover tightly and allow to marinate at room temperature for at least 2 hours. If marinating longer, refrigerate.

3) Stir in the vinegar within 15 minutes of serving. Sprinkle on the walnuts at the very last minute. This recipe can be served cold or at room temperature.

~ Yield: 6 servings ~

Braised Brussels Sprouts
in Maple Mustard Sauce

Brussels sprouts come in a range of sizes. I usually like to cut the larger ones so they won't be too imposing a mouthful. If they're not too large, you can just cut them in half. But if they're golf ball size, quarter them. (And if they're tiny, just leave them whole.)

NOTE:
♥ A high-grade maple syrup (one with very subtle flavor) works best for this.

2 tablespoons extra-virgin olive oil
¼ cup minced onion
4 cups (1 pound) Brussels sprouts,
   halved or quartered lengthwise
   (or left whole, if tiny)

½ teaspoon salt (or to taste)
4 to 6 tablespoons water
¼ cup Dijon mustard
2 tablespoons real maple syrup
Freshly ground black pepper, to taste

1) Place a medium-sized skillet over medium heat. After about a minute, add the olive oil and swirl to coat the pan.

2) Add the onion and sauté for 3 to 5 minutes, or until it begins to soften. Add the Brussels sprouts and salt, and sauté for 5 minutes.

3) Sprinkle in 4 tablespoons water, shake the pan, and cover. Cook over medium heat for about 5 to 8 minutes, or until the Brussels sprouts are bright green and fork-tender. (You might need to add another tablespoon or two of water during this time to prevent sticking. Just keep your eye on it—and your fork intermittently in it.)

4) Using a small whisk in a medium-small bowl, beat together the mustard and maple syrup until smooth. Add this mixture to the pan and stir to combine.

5) Serve hot, warm, or at room temperature, topped with a shower of fresh black pepper, if desired.

Two slight variations. You could:
1) Cook it longer in the glaze, so everything melds deeply. The flavors will intensify and the sprouts will become softer. (They will, however, lose their color.)
2) Instead of adding the glaze directly to the pan, serve the braised sprouts with the glaze drizzled over the top. This is prettier, but the flavor will have infused less.

~ Yield: 4 to 5 servings ~

Brussels Sprouts

with Shallots and Hazelnuts

Brussels sprouts are on my short list of vegetables that I prefer a little on the well-done side rather than the more fashionable "tender-crisp." In this case, I like them almost scorched on the outside and buttery soft on the inside.

NOTES:
- ♥ To blanch hazelnuts, spread them out on a tray and roast in a 250°F oven for 5 to 10 minutes, or until fragrant. Remove from the oven, cool on the tray, and then rub off the skins with your fingers or in a clean tea towel.
- ♥ The roasted hazelnut oil is a really nice touch, if you can get hold of some.
- ♥ Butter is a nice alternative to olive oil for this recipe.

> 1 tablespoon extra-virgin olive oil or unsalted butter
> 1 cup minced shallots (about 6 ounces)
> 4 cups (1 pound) Brussels sprouts, halved or quartered lengthwise
>   (or left whole, if small)
> ½ teaspoon salt (or to taste)
> Roasted hazelnut oil (optional)
> Freshly ground black pepper, to taste
> ½ cup (or more) blanched hazelnuts, coarsely chopped

1) Put up a large saucepan of water to boil.

2) In the meantime, place a large, deep skillet over medium heat. After about a minute, add the olive oil or melt the butter and swirl to coat the pan. Stir in the shallots, and cook, stirring frequently, for about 3 to 5 minutes, or until the shallots turn a deep golden color.

3) When the water from step 1 boils, turn the heat down to low and add the Brussels sprouts. Simmer for 2 to 3 minutes, or until the sprouts turn bright green and shiny and are beginning to become tender.

4) Dump the sprouts into a colander in the sink, then refresh under cold running water. Drain well.

5) Add the sprouts to the shallots, sprinkling in the salt. Stir until well combined, then spread the vegetables out to the edges of the pan to make a shallow layer.

6) Turn the heat up for a few minutes, shaking the pan a few times to redistribute the heat. This allows the juices to evaporate—and slightly scorches the vegetables—both of which serve to intensify the flavor.

7) Serve hot or warm, with a light drizzle of roasted hazelnut oil, if available, and with sprinklings of black pepper and chopped hazelnuts.

~ Yield: 4 to 5 servings ~

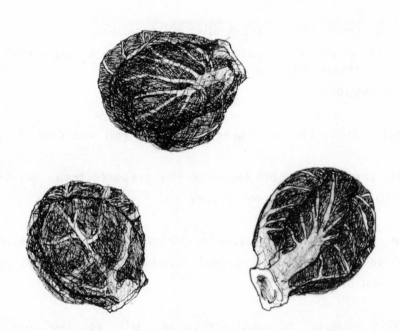

❧ crispy-edged ❧
Roasted Brussels Sprouts

If you think you dislike Brussels sprouts, think again. Or don't think at all—just go get some and roast and eat them. By then, everything will likely have changed. Pleasantly crusty on the outside and soft and savory on the inside, roasted Brussels sprouts are a revelation. Added bonus: The outer leaves that invariably fall off during the baking process will crispen into little "chips."

NOTE:
♥ These will keep for up to 5 days in a tightly covered container in the refrigerator.

> 1 tablespoon extra-virgin olive oil (possibly more)
> 4 cups (1 pound) Brussels sprouts, halved or quartered lengthwise
> (or left whole, if small)
> Salt (optional)

1) Preheat the oven to 425°F. Line a baking tray with foil and coat it with oil.

2) Place the Brussels sprouts cut-side down on the prepared tray, moving them around so that all the cut surfaces touch some of the oil.

3) Place the tray in the center of the oven for 10 minutes. At this point, shake the tray and/or use tongs to redistribute the sprouts so that more surfaces can come into contact with the hot oil.

4) Roast for another 5 minutes, or until a taste test tells you the sprouts are done to your liking. (They will cook a little further from their own heat after they come out of the oven.)

5) Remove the tray from the oven and let the sprouts cool for about 10 minutes on the baking tray. You can salt them lightly during this time, if you wish. Serve hot, warm, or at room temperature.

~ Yield: 4 servings ~

⊚Brussels Sprouts⊚
⊚ ⊚ ⊚ Pickles ⊚ ⊚ ⊚

Not your run-of-the-mill condiment! These are really fun to snack upon.

NOTES:
- ♥ This recipe needs a minimum 4-hour pickling period, but a longer sit will make the pickles even better. They will keep for 2 weeks or longer.
- ♥ Seasoned rice vinegar, lightly salted and sweetened, is available in Asian grocery stores and in the imported foods section of good supermarkets.

> ½ pound Brussels sprouts
> 1 tablespoon light-colored honey
> ⅔ cup hot water
> ⅓ cup seasoned rice vinegar

1) Put up a large saucepan of water to boil.

2) In the meantime, trim the ends from the Brussels sprouts, and if they are large, cut them in half. If they're very large, quarter them. If they're small, you can leave them whole. You should have about 2 cups.

3) When the water boils, add the sprouts and lower the heat to a simmer. Cook for 1 to 2 minutes, until tender-crisp, and then drain into a colander in the sink. Refresh under cold running water for a minute or so, then drain again.

4) Place the honey in a medium-sized bowl and add the hot water. Stir until the honey dissolves, then add the vinegar and mix well.

5) Add the Brussels sprouts, making sure they are completely submerged so they can "pickle." Let sit at room temperature for about 20 minutes, then transfer to a jar with a tight-fitting lid and refrigerate.

~ Yield: 4 to 5 servings ~

◊ Chile Cabbage ◊
with Shiitakes, Sweet-Crisp Onions, & Tofu

A three-stage cooking process (same pan, no cleaning in between) allows each ingredient to reach optimal texture and maximum flavor.

> 2 to 3 tablespoons canola or peanut oil
> 16 medium shiitake mushrooms (about 10 ounces),
>   stemmed and very thinly sliced
> 2 medium jalapeños, cut into thin rounds
> ¼ teaspoon salt
> 6 cups cut green cabbage (1-inch "squares")
> 2 tablespoons soy sauce
> 1 tablespoon cider vinegar
> 1½ teaspoons Chinese-style dark sesame oil (plus extra)
> 1½ coarsely chopped onions (¾-inch "squares")
> 10 ounces very firm tofu

1) Place a large, deep skillet over medium heat. After about a minute, add 1 tablespoon of the oil and swirl to coat the pan. Add the mushrooms and stir-fry over medium-high heat for 5 minutes. Stir in the jalapeños, plus ⅛ teaspoon of the salt, and cook, stirring frequently, for 5 to 8 minutes longer, or until the mushrooms are very limp.

2) Push the mushrooms and jalapeños to one side of the pan, then add another tablespoon of oil to the exposed surface, followed by the cabbage and another ⅛ teaspoon of the salt.

3) Keeping the heat medium-high, stir-fry the cabbage only for about 3 minutes, then mix in the sidelined mushrooms and jalapeños. Spread out the mixture, cover the pan, and let it steam (okay if it scorches slightly) for about 5 minutes. Scrape the bottom of the pan and mix intermittently.

4) In a small bowl, combine the soy sauce, vinegar, and sesame oil, then pour this in. Mix well, cover, and continue to cook over low heat for another 5 to 8 minutes, or until done to your liking. Transfer to a serving bowl and set aside.

5) Without cleaning it, return the pan to the stove over medium heat. Wait about a minute, then add a little oil and swirl to coat the pan. Turn up the heat to high and flash-cook the onions, shaking the pan, for only about 1 to 2 minutes, or until the onions become shiny and golden on the edges but are still crunchy. Add these to the cabbage mixture in the bowl.

6) Return the uncleaned pan to medium heat one more time, wait another minute, add another little bit of oil, and swirl to coat the pan. Add the tofu in a single layer (okay if touching) and cook undisturbed for about 5 minutes on each side, or until crisp and deep golden brown. Toss into the cabbage mixture and serve. Pass around the sesame oil, so people can add a little extra, if they wish.

~ Yield: 4 to 6 servings ~

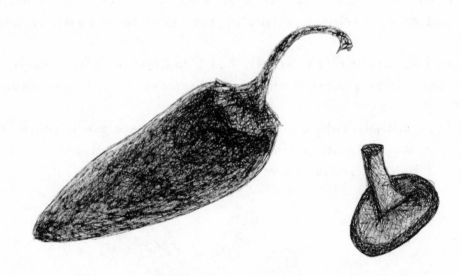

Sesame-Braised Cabbage with Leeks

Gentle and soothing, this lovely dish is more complex and satisfying than you might expect.

NOTE:
♥ Leeks are easy to clean. Rinse the outsides to get rid of any mud, then slice the white and light green parts and place them in a big bowl of water. Swish around vigorously, then lift out the leeks with your hands or a slotted spoon, leaving the dirt in the bottom of the bowl of water.

> 1 tablespoon unsalted butter
> 4 cups sliced leeks (whites and as much of the greens as feasible)
> ¼ teaspoon salt (possibly more)
> 4 cups cut green cabbage (1-inch "squares")
> Freshly ground black pepper, to taste
> Chinese-style dark sesame oil
> Toasted sesame seeds

1) Melt the butter in a Dutch oven or large, deep skillet over medium heat. Add the leeks and salt, and cook, stirring occasionally, for about 10 minutes, or until very tender.

2) Add the cabbage and stir to combine. Add 2 tablespoons water, cover, reduce the heat to low, and cook, stirring occasionally, until the cabbage is tender, about 20 minutes.

3) Season to taste with freshly ground black pepper and a pinch more salt if needed. Serve hot or warm, drizzled with a tiny bit of dark sesame oil and topped with a generous sprinkling of lightly toasted sesame seeds.

~ Yield: 4 servings ~

Sweet & Sour Red Cabbage
WITH Berries

Adding fruit to vegetables isn't as unusual as it might seem. Fruit is used in many savory meat and vegetable dishes in many ethnic cuisines. In this northern-European-influenced combination, blueberries and cranberries are the guest stars, blending in incredibly well. And the color is just gorgeous!

NOTE:
♥ This tastes better the day after you make it, and better yet the day after that. It freezes beautifully as well. Leave the blueberries out until you reheat and are ready to serve (to preserve their pretty shape).

> 2 tablespoons canola oil
> 1½ cups minced onion
> 8 cups cut red cabbage (1-inch "squares")
> 2 tablespoons red wine vinegar
> 2 tablespoons balsamic vinegar
> ½ teaspoon salt (or to taste)
> ⅔ cup dried cranberries
> 1 to 2 cups blueberries (fresh or unsweetened frozen, defrosted)
> Freshly ground black pepper, to taste

1) Place a large, deep skillet over medium heat. After about a minute, add the canola oil and swirl to coat the pan. Add the onion and sauté for about 5 minutes, or until translucent. Add the cabbage and stir well so that it gets completely coated with oil.

2) Reduce the heat to medium-low, stir in the vinegars, and cover the pan. Continue to cook, stirring occasionally, until nicely wilted, 10 to 15 minutes.

3) Turn the heat down to low, then stir in the salt and dried cranberries. Cover and continue cooking for 20 to 30 minutes, or until the cabbage is very tender. (If the cabbage seems dry at any time, you can add a few tablespoons of water.)

4) Stir in the blueberries, then taste to see if more salt might be needed. Add black pepper to taste—and even a bit more red wine vinegar (for tartness) or balsamic vinegar (for sweeter tartness) if you like. Serve hot or warm.

~ Yield: 4 to 6 servings ~

STIR-FRIED CARROTS, RED PEPPERS, & RED ONIONS
with ROASTED CASHEWS

Bright, warm colors are just the beginning of this cheerful experience, which only gets better with each crunchy bite.

NOTE:
- ♥ Have all the vegetables cut and ready near the stove. The cooking goes pretty fast, and you want to move it along once you get started.

> 1 cup whole cashews
> 2 tablespoons canola oil or peanut oil
> 1 large red onion (about ¾ pound), cut into large chunks
> 1½ pounds carrots (6 medium), in thick (¼-inch) diagonal slices
> 1 tablespoon minced fresh ginger (optional)
> ¼ teaspoon salt
> 1 teaspoon minced or crushed garlic
> 1 large red bell pepper (about ½ pound), in 1-inch squares
> 3 tablespoons balsamic vinegar
> 1 tablespoon soy sauce
> Red pepper flakes, to taste (optional)
> 1 cup pineapple chunks, fresh or canned, packed in juice, drained (optional)

1) Preheat the oven to 300°F. Spread the cashews in a single layer on a baking tray and place in the center of the oven. Roast until golden (about 10 minutes), shaking the pan every now and then. Remove the tray from the oven and set it aside.

2) Place a large wok over medium heat. After about a minute, add the oil and swirl to coat the pan. Turn the heat to high and add the onion, carrots, and ginger, if desired. Sprinkle with salt and stir-fry for about 5 minutes or until the carrot begins to become tender.

3) Toss in the garlic and red pepper pieces, and continue to cook over high heat for another 5 minutes. Add the vinegar and soy sauce and cook for about 2 minutes longer.

4) Add red pepper flakes to taste, if desired, and serve hot or warm, topped with the cashews and garnished, if you wish, with pineapple.

~ Yield: 4 to 5 servings ~

COCONUT ~ GINGER CARROTS

...a sublime, Caribbean-inspired gratin.

> 2 tablespoons extra-virgin olive oil
> 1½ cups minced onion
> 1 heaping tablespoon minced fresh ginger
> 2 teaspoons minced or crushed garlic
> ½ teaspoon salt
> 2 pounds carrots, peeled and cut on the diagonal into ¼-inch-thick slices
> 2 tablespoons fresh lemon or lime juice
> ½ cup minced crystallized ginger (optional)
> ½ cup shredded unsweetened coconut

1) Preheat the oven to 375°F. Coat the bottom surface of a 1½-quart gratin pan with 1 tablespoon of the oil and set aside.

2) Place a large, deep skillet over medium heat. After about a minute, add the remaining olive oil and swirl to coat the pan. Add the onion and ginger and sauté for 5 minutes. Stir in the garlic and half the salt and sauté for another 5 minutes.

3) Add the carrots and the remaining salt, and stir until the carrots are well coated with the onion mixture. Turn down the heat, cover the pan, and cook undisturbed for 5 minutes. Add the lemon juice and crystallized ginger, if desired. Cover again and cook for 5 minutes longer.

4) Transfer the mixture to the prepared pan, cover tightly with foil, and bake for 15 to 20 minutes, or until the carrots are fork-tender.

5) Uncover, sprinkle with the coconut (making sure it gets into all the crevices), and return to the oven until the coconut is golden, 10 minutes or longer. Serve hot or warm.

~ Yield: 5 to 6 servings ~

Coated Carrots
Afrique du Nord

A good dose of cumin (both whole and ground), cinnamon, and garlic team up with citrus to coat these carrots clear into otherworldliness.

NOTES:
- ♥ This dish starts on the stovetop and finishes in the oven, but it's not a lot of work.
- ♥ The optional butter goes a long way for flavor.

Nonstick cooking spray for the pan
2 tablespoons extra-virgin olive oil
½ teaspoon cumin seeds
2 teaspoons ground cumin
1 teaspoon cinnamon
1 teaspoon unsalted butter (optional)
1 teaspoon minced or crushed garlic
2 pounds carrots (about 10 medium carrots), peeled and cut on the diagonal into ¼-inch slices
½ teaspoon salt (or to taste)
2 tablespoons orange juice (fresh, if possible)
2 tablespoons fresh lemon juice

OPTIONAL GARNISHES:
- ♥ Additional lemon juice (and/or lemon wedges)
- ♥ A touch of honey
- ♥ Minced fresh mint (highly recommended!)
- ♥ Red pepper flakes

1) Preheat the oven to 400°F. Line a baking tray with foil, and spray generously with nonstick spray.

2) Place a large, deep skillet over medium heat. After about a minute, add the olive oil and swirl to coat the pan.

3) Sprinkle in the cumin seeds, and toss the pan a few times. Let the seeds brown over medium heat for about 3 minutes, taking care that they don't burn. When the seeds give off a toasty aroma, add the ground cumin and cinnamon and cook the spices alone for a few minutes longer.

4) Melt in the butter, if desired, then stir in the garlic. Add the carrots, turning them until thoroughly coated with the spices. Sprinkle in the salt and orange juice, and stir well. Cover and cook over medium heat for about 5 minutes, stirring several times. Transfer the mixture, including all the coating, to the prepared baking tray, spreading everything into a single layer.

5) Place the tray in the center of the oven for 15 minutes, visiting the mixture once or twice during this time to shake the pan and/or turn over the carrots with tongs.

6) Remove the tray from the oven, and let the mixture cool on the tray for about 5 minutes before transferring to a bowl. Add the lemon juice and sprinkle with any or all of the optional additions. Serve hot, warm, or at room temperature.

△ △

~ Yield: 4 to 5 servings ~

Cauliflower~Cheese
꒰꒰꒰꒰ Appetizer ꜱꜱꜱꜱ

A wonderful first course on its own, this tasty little dish is also a versatile side.

NOTE:
- ♥ You can make this a day or two ahead. It keeps very well in a tightly covered container in the refrigerator, and the flavors will deepen.

> 1 medium-large cauliflower (about 2 pounds)
> 3 tablespoons extra-virgin olive oil
> 1 teaspoon cumin seeds
> 1 cup thinly sliced onion
> 1/4 teaspoon salt
> 1 teaspoon minced or crushed garlic
> 1 tablespoon red wine vinegar or cider vinegar
> Freshly ground black pepper, to taste
> 1 cup diced mild white cheese (Jack, fontina, or something similar)
> 3 to 4 tablespoons sour cream or plain yogurt (optional)

1) Put up a large saucepan of water to boil, or boil some water in the bottom section of a vegetable steamer. In the meantime, trim the cauliflower of its base and leaves and cut or break the rest into 3/4-inch florets. (You should get about 6 cups.)

2) Cook the cauliflower in—or steam over—simmering water until just tender (2 to 3 minutes in the water; 5 or more minutes in the steamer). Refresh in a colander under cold running water and drain thoroughly. Transfer to a medium-sized bowl.

3) Place a medium-small skillet over medium heat. After about a minute, add the olive oil and swirl to coat the pan.

4) Add the cumin seeds and cook over medium heat for about 2 to 3 minutes, or until aromatic. Don't let them burn! Add the onion and salt, turn the heat to medium-low, and cook for about 5 to 8 minutes, or until the onion becomes very soft. Stir in the garlic and remove from the heat.

5) Add the sautéed onion mixture to the cauliflower, scraping in every last drop of oil. Stir in the vinegar and some black pepper, then add the cheese and optional sour cream or yogurt. Mix until thoroughly combined and taste to adjust the seasonings. You can serve this right away, but for optimal flavor, I recommend covering the bowl and letting it stand for at least an hour before serving. Serve at room temperature or chilled.

~ Yield: 4 to 5 servings ~

Cauliflower Gratin
with Capers and Bread Crumbs

Equally good—and nutty in different ways—when made with Parmesan or with a Swiss cheese, such as Emmenthaler.

NOTE:
- ♥ Make your own bread crumbs by drying out some of your favorite bread, then crumbling it either by hand (in a plastic bag, so it won't go all over the place) or in a food processor with the steel blade (a few spurts).

> 2 tablespoons extra-virgin olive oil
> 1 medium-large cauliflower (about 1¾ pounds)
> 1 cup chopped onion
> 1 to 2 tablespoons capers, drained
> ½ cup fine bread crumbs
> ¼ cup grated Parmesan or Swiss cheese
> Freshly ground black pepper, to taste

1) Preheat the oven to 425°F. Line a large baking tray with foil and brush it with 1 tablespoon of the olive oil. Coat the bottom surface of a 1½-quart gratin pan with the other tablespoon of oil and set aside.

2) Cut or break the cauliflower into ¾-inch florets (you should get about 6 cups) and spread them on the baking tray. Roast in the center of the oven for 10 minutes.

3) Shake the tray to loosen the cauliflower, then sprinkle on the onion and capers and roast for another 10 minutes. Remove the tray from the oven and transfer all of the cooked vegetables to the prepared gratin pan.

4) Combine the bread crumbs and cheese, and sprinkle this mixture over the top. Let it sit until shortly before serving, then place the gratin pan under a preheated broiler for 5 to 8 minutes, or until the top is crisp and brown. (Watch it carefully! It can burn in a heartbeat.) Serve hot, warm, or at room temperature. Add pepper to taste.

~ Yield: 3 to 4 servings ~

Cauliflower & Red Onion MUSTARD PICKLES

The onions turn bright pink and stay that way, making this pickle combination especially beautiful.

NOTE:
- ♥ Seasoned rice vinegar, lightly salted and sweetened, is available in Asian grocery stores and in the imported foods section of good supermarkets.

> ½ medium red onion, cut in thin slices (about 1 cup)
> 1 medium cauliflower (about 1½ pounds) in 1-inch florets
>   (4 cups florets)
> ⅓ cup seasoned rice vinegar
> ⅔ cup water
> ¼ cup Dijon mustard

1) Place the onion in a colander in the sink.

2) Put up a large saucepan of water to boil. Add the cauliflower and turn the heat down to a simmer. Cook the cauliflower until just tender, 2 to 3 minutes, then pour it, water and all, into the colander, dousing the onion in the process. Drain well.

3) Combine the vinegar, water, and mustard in a medium-sized bowl. Add the cauliflower and onion, mixing gently until all the vegetables are in contact with the marinade.

4) Let sit at room temperature for about 20 minutes, then transfer to a container with a tight-fitting lid and refrigerate. The pickles will be ready in about 4 hours, but a longer sit will make them even better. They will keep for about 2 weeks or longer.

~ Yield: 4 to 5 servings ~

CILANTRO-WALNUT PESTO

Pesto doesn't always have to be basil-flavored. This tart, pungent version, made with cilantro, is so good and versatile, I keep some in my refrigerator pretty much all the time and never get tired of it.

NOTES:
- ♥ I say "mostly stemmed" for the cilantro, so you won't be fussing with stemming it for hours. Just do your best to get mostly leaves into the pesto, and if a few stems get in too, no big deal.
- ♥ The walnuts do not need to be toasted, but you can experiment with toasting them lightly to see if you prefer the slightly enhanced flavor.
- ♥ Spoon the pesto into hot soups and onto grilled burgers of any persuasion. It will keep for a week or longer in a tightly covered container in the refrigerator. A thin layer of olive oil across the top will help preserve it.

> 3 packed cups cilantro (mostly stemmed) (about 10 ounces)
> 1 to 2 small cloves garlic
> 1 cup walnuts (toasting optional)
> ¼ teaspoon salt
> 2 teaspoons fresh lemon juice
> 6 to 8 tablespoons extra-virgin olive oil

1) Place the cilantro, garlic, walnuts, and salt in a food processor fitted with the steel blade. Pulse until pulverized, adding the lemon juice as you go.

2) Run the processor again, drizzling the olive oil in a steady stream. When it reaches the consistency that looks right to you, stop the machine. Transfer the pesto to a small container with a tight-fitting lid.

3) Smooth the top of the pesto with the back of a spoon and add a thin layer of olive oil to cover the top. Cover and chill. Serve as desired.

~ Yield: 1 cup ~

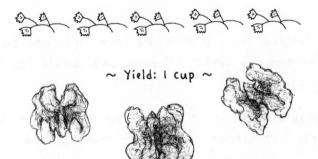

Southwest Summer
CORN HASH

One trip to the farmers market in August or September can lead to small, great things, such as this simple dish. Try it as a side for dinner (it goes with everything!) or next to your breakfast eggs, accompanied by a few thick slices of vine-ripened tomatoes (in addition to the optional sweet cherry tomatoes, which I hope you'll include).

NOTE:
♥ The optional butter goes a long way for flavor.

> 1 tablespoon extra-virgin olive oil
> 1 cup minced onion
> ½ cup minced poblano chile (about half a medium chile)
> 1 teaspoon ground cumin
> About 1 teaspoon unsalted butter (optional)
> 2 ears freshly shorn sweet corn (about 2 cups)
> 1 small zucchini, diced (optional)
> 1 cup minced red bell pepper (1 small pepper)
> ¼ teaspoon salt (rounded measure)
> 1 teaspoon minced or crushed garlic
> Freshly ground black pepper, to taste
>
> OPTIONAL EXTRAS:
> ♥ 1 to 2 scallions, very finely minced
> ♥ About 10 fresh basil leaves, in thin strips
> ♥ Up to a dozen very sweet, small cherry tomatoes, halved
> ♥ A touch of grated mild cheese or sour cream

1) Place a large, deep skillet over medium heat. After about a minute, add the olive oil and swirl to coat the pan.

2) Add the onion, chile, and cumin to the oil, and sauté for 5 minutes, or until the onion becomes soft.

3) Melt in the butter, if desired, then stir in the corn, optional zucchini, and bell pepper. Sprinkle in the salt and add the garlic, stirring well. Sauté for another 5 to 8 minutes or so, or until done to your liking.

4) Grind in some black pepper and stir in any of the optional extras. (You can also use these as toppings.) Serve hot, warm, or at room temperature.

~ Yield: 4 to 5 servings (a little more if adding the zucchini and tomatoes) ~

fresh corn, black bean, & avocado Saladita

A cheerful, uncooked summer preparation resembling a relish or a salsa, this makes a nice little side dish as well as a great topping for fish or vegetable burgers.

NOTES:
- The seemingly many ingredients are actually just tossed together, so labor is minimal. You can make all of this (short of adding the avocado) up to two days ahead of time, if you cover it and keep it in the refrigerator.
- Try this as a lunch entrée, stuffed into hollowed-out cucumbers or bell peppers, surrounded by tortilla chips.

2 ears freshly shorn sweet corn (about 2 cups)
3 tablespoons fresh lime juice
3 tablespoons extra-virgin olive oil
1 15-ounce can (1 3/4 cups) black beans, rinsed and drained
1 cup diced halved cherry tomatoes (the sweetest ones possible)
1/4 cup minced red bell pepper
3 tablespoons very finely minced poblano chile
1/4 teaspoon (rounded measure) minced garlic
3 tablespoons very finely minced red onion
1/4 teaspoon salt
3 tablespoons minced cilantro
1/2 cup crumbled feta cheese (about 4 ounces)
Freshly ground black pepper, to taste
2 medium (or 3 small) firm-but-ripe avocados, in tiny dice

1) In a medium-large bowl, combine all the ingredients except the avocados, and mix well. Cover and let marinate for at least an hour before serving. (This can be done at room temperature, if the weather is not too hot. Otherwise, refrigerate.)

2) Gently stir in the avocado dice about 15 minutes or so before serving. Correct black pepper to taste. Serve cold or at room temperature.

~ Yield: About 6 servings ~

Feta-Walnut-Stuffed Cucumbers

Serve these for lunch, with soup, or as an appetizer or side dish for dinner.

> 1 cup walnuts (not toasted)
> 1 handful of fresh parsley
> 1 cup crumbled feta cheese
> ½ cup milk
> ½ teaspoon minced or crushed garlic
> 1 teaspoon mild paprika (plus extra)
> ⅛ teaspoon cayenne
> 3 to 4 medium-sized cucumbers

1) Combine the walnuts and parsley in a blender or food processor and pulverize to a powdery state with a series of pulses.

2) Add all the remaining ingredients except the cucumbers and purée until smooth.

3) Peel the cucumbers, if desired, and cut them in half lengthwise. Use a spoon to scrape out the seeds, then fill the cavities with the feta-walnut mixture, patting it into place with a fork or spoon (or your hands). Use more or less filling for each, depending on the size of the cucumbers and how full you would like them.

4) Dust the tops lightly with a little extra paprika and serve cold or at room temperature. If you would like to serve them cold, place the filled cucumbers on a plate, cover tightly with plastic wrap, and refrigerate for up to 4 hours before serving. Don't let them sit too much longer than that.

~ Yield: About 4 servings ~

Eggplant, Green Beans, Pumpkin, and Basil
in Coconut-Tomato Curry

Welcome to one of my all-time favorite vegetable mélanges!

NOTES:
- ♥ Look for the Thai ingredients (Thai Kitchen brand) in the international foods section of your supermarket.
- ♥ Kabocha squash is a Japanese pumpkin. If you can find it, you will love it! If you can't find it, you will also love butternut squash.
- ♥ Eat this as a stew or chunky soup, or serve it over rice. (If choosing the latter, put up some jasmine rice or brown basmati rice to cook before you begin.)
- ♥ Use a flavorful vegetable broth, such as Imagine brand.
- ♥ For best results, cook the squash ahead of time (by steaming or blanching) until almost tender.
- ♥ This dish will keep for up to 5 days in a tightly covered container in the refrigerator. It reheats beautifully.

2 teaspoons red curry paste
1½ to 2 tablespoons minced fresh ginger
1 (14-ounce) can light coconut milk (about 1¾ cups)
1½ cups vegetable broth
2 tablespoons fish sauce ("nam pla") or 1 to 2 tablespoons soy sauce
1 tablespoon brown sugar (optional)
1 (15-ounce) can diced tomatoes (about 1¾ cups tomatoes-plus-liquid)
1 small (5- to 6-ounce) Japanese or Chinese eggplant, cut into ½-inch-thick half-rounds
2 cups (about 10 ounces) diced kabocha or butternut squash, steamed or blanched until almost tender
2 cups (about 8 ounces) green beans, trimmed and cut into 2-inch lengths
20 to 25 fresh basil leaves (Thai basil, if available)

1) Measure the curry paste and ginger into a large saucepan, then add the coconut milk and broth, and whisk until smooth. Bring to a boil over high heat, reduce the heat, and simmer, covered, for 15 minutes.

2) Stir in the fish or soy sauce and brown sugar, if desired.

3) Add the tomatoes, eggplant, squash, and green beans. Bring to a boil, then reduce the heat and simmer, partially covered, for about 10 minutes, or until the vegetables are tender. Stir in the basil leaves (whole or torn in half) and serve hot, over rice.

~ Yield: 5 to 6 servings ~

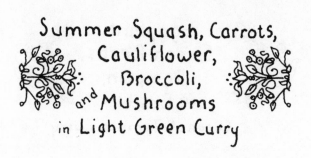

Summer Squash, Carrots, Cauliflower, Broccoli, and Mushrooms in Light Green Curry

The vegetables are bathed in a subtle sauce that delivers a delayed effect: soothing at first, and then slightly edgy, with a terrific aftertaste.

NOTES:
- ♥ Look for the Thai ingredients (Thai Kitchen brand) in the "international" section of your supermarket.
- ♥ Eat this as a stew or chunky soup, or serve it over rice. (If choosing the latter, put up some jasmine rice or brown basmati rice to cook before you begin.)
- ♥ Use a flavorful vegetable broth, such as Imagine brand.

> 2 teaspoons green curry paste
> 1 (14-ounce) can light coconut milk (about 1¾ cups)
> 1½ cups vegetable broth
> A 4-inch piece of lemongrass, cut in two, then split lengthwise
>   (or 2 teaspoons grated lemon zest)
> 2 to 3 tablespoons Thai fish sauce ("nam pla")
>   —or 2 to 3 tablespoons soy sauce
> 1 small yellow summer squash (about 4 ounces), cut into ½-inch-thick
>   half-rounds
> 1 small zucchini (about 4 ounces), cut into ½-inch-thick half-rounds
> 2 cups small (½-inch) cauliflower florets
> 2 cups small (½-inch) broccoli florets
> 1 medium carrot, in ¼-inch diagonal slices
> ½ pound small, tight mushrooms, cleaned and stemmed
>   (halved or left whole, depending on the size)
> ⅓ cup minced fresh cilantro
> ½ cup toasted cashews (optional)

1) Measure the curry paste into a medium-large saucepan, then add the coconut milk and broth, and whisk until smooth.

2) Add the lemongrass or lemon zest. Bring to a boil over high heat, then reduce the heat and simmer, covered, for 15 minutes.

3) Remove and discard the lemongrass stalk, if using. Stir in the fish sauce or soy sauce. Add the squash, zucchini, cauliflower, broccoli, carrot, and mushroom caps, and bring to a boil. Reduce the heat and simmer, partially covered, for about 10 minutes, or until the vegetables are just tender. Add the cilantro at the very last minute, then serve hot—plain, in a bowl, or over rice, topped with cashews, if desired.

~ Yield: 5 to 6 servings ~

Grilled Eggplant and Portobello Mushrooms
with Miso-Apple-Wasabi Glaze

You will need a quick trip to an Asian grocery store to pick up the shiro miso and the wasabi (green horseradish paste). While you're there, if you can find some shiso (Japanese fresh green herb) I recommend you buy some of that, too—it's amazing stuff! But this recipe is wonderful without it as well.

NOTES:
- ♥ You can make the glaze well in advance—it keeps in the refrigerator for weeks.
- ♥ No need to peel the eggplant if the skin is shiny and tight.

> 4 tablespoons shiro miso (the very light, beige-colored type)
> 4 tablespoons apple juice
> 1/8 teaspoon minced or crushed garlic
> 1/2 teaspoon grated fresh ginger
> 1/4 teaspoon prepared wasabi
> Canola oil or peanut oil
> 1 large globe eggplant (about 1 3/4 pounds), cut into 3/4-inch rounds
> 6 portobello mushrooms, about 4 inches in diameter, stems removed
> Salt and freshly ground black pepper, to taste
> 5 to 6 shiso leaves, minced (optional)

1) In a medium-small bowl, combine the miso, apple juice, garlic, ginger, and wasabi, and whisk until smooth. Set aside.

2) Preheat the broiler. Line a large baking tray with foil and brush it with oil.

3) Cut the eggplant slices and mushroom caps in half and arrange the pieces on the tray. Brush the eggplant with a light coating of oil and sprinkle a bit of salt over all.

4) Broil, with the surface of the eggplant and mushrooms about 4 inches below the heat source, until the eggplant is dark golden brown, 3 to 4 minutes. (Watch carefully—all broilers are different and what is golden this minute can be charcoal the next! Don't answer the phone!)

5) Use tongs to turn the vegetables over and continue broiling on the other side until the eggplant is dark golden brown and soft, about 3 to 4 minutes more.

Stir-Fried Eggplant with Ginger-Plum Sauce

NOTES:

♥ No need to peel the eggplant if the skin is shiny and tight.

♥ The eggplant will want to stick a bit to the pan, even with a nice coating of oil, so use a flexible spatula when stirring and be sure to scrape the bottom of the pan often.

⅓ cup plum jam (leaving the largest chunks of plum in the jar for another use)

2 teaspoons Dijon mustard

½ teaspoon very finely grated fresh ginger

Salt and freshly ground black pepper, to taste

2 large eggplants (about 3 pounds)

2 tablespoons canola oil or peanut oil

¼ teaspoon salt

Red pepper flakes, to taste (optional)

1) In a small bowl, combine the plum jam, mustard, and ginger, and stir until well combined. Season to taste with a dash of salt and some freshly ground black pepper, and set aside.

2) Cut the eggplants lengthwise into ½-inch-thick slices, then crosswise into ½-inch-thick sticks.

3) Place a large, deep skillet or wok over medium heat. After about a minute, add the oil and swirl to coat the pan. Add the eggplants and salt, and cook, stirring continuously and scraping the bottom of the pan often, for 10 to 15 minutes, or until the eggplant is golden brown, very tender, and has collapsed in volume by about half. (If the eggplant seems to be browning more quickly than it is becoming tender, reduce the heat to medium-low and/or add a splash of water.)

4) Remove from the heat, add the plum sauce, and stir to combine. Season to taste with additional salt, if needed, and some freshly ground black pepper. Serve hot, warm, or at room temperature, topped with red pepper flakes, if desired.

~ Yield: 3 to 4 servings ~

6) Turn the slices over once again and brush (or spoon) the top surface with a generous coating of the glaze. Return to the broiler for another 2 to 3 minutes, or until the glaze bubbles a little and acquires a few golden brown spots.

7) Serve hot, warm, or at room temperature, with extra glaze if you like and a few grinds of black pepper. Garnish with a sprinkling of minced shiso leaves, if available.

~ Yield: 4 servings (3 mushroom halves and 3 to 4 eggplant slices per person) ~

TUNISIAN EGGPLANT

A great appetizer, scooped up with endive or other vegetables or spread on crackers, this recipe also can be used as a relish on top of any grilled tofu, chicken, or fish. It even goes well tossed with hot pasta!

NOTE:
- ❤ No need to peel the eggplant if the skin is shiny and tight.

> 2 tablespoons extra-virgin olive oil
> 1½ cups minced onion
> 1½ pounds eggplant, cut into ½-inch cubes
> ½ teaspoon salt (possibly more, to taste)
> 1 teaspoon minced or crushed garlic
> 3 tablespoons tomato paste
> ¼ cup red wine vinegar
> 1 cup pitted green olives, chopped
> 1 small jar (6 ounces) marinated artichoke hearts
> Pinches of dried tarragon, basil, and oregano, to taste
> Freshly ground black pepper, to taste

1) Place a large, deep skillet over medium heat. After about a minute, add the olive oil and swirl to coat the pan. Add the onions and sauté for 5 to 8 minutes, or until soft and translucent.

2) Stir in the eggplant, salt, and garlic, then cover the pan. Reduce the heat to medium-low and cook until the eggplant is very soft (about 15 minutes). Add small amounts of water, a tablespoon at a time, if the eggplant appears to be sticking.

3) Stir in the tomato paste and vinegar, and heat just to boiling. Remove from the heat right away and stir in the olives.

4) Drain the artichoke hearts, discarding the liquid. Cut each piece into 2 to 3 smaller pieces. Stir these into the mixture, then allow it all to cool to room temperature.

5) Add the dried herbs and black pepper to taste. Serve at room temperature or cold.

~ Yield: About 6 servings ~

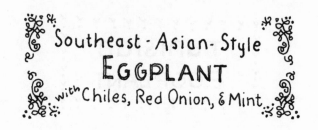

Southeast-Asian-Style
EGGPLANT
with Chiles, Red Onion, & Mint

Eggplant gets yet another opportunity to showcase its flavor-absorbing talent. And these are flavors well worth absorbing!

NOTES:
- ♥ Serrano chiles are the small, tight-skinned green or red ones often used in Thai cooking. They're quite hot, and most of the heat is concentrated in the seeds and inner membranes. Wash your hands and all cutting surfaces with soap and warm water immediately afterward! And if you can't find fresh serranos, substitute jalapeños, or just add red pepper flakes to taste.
- ♥ No need to peel the eggplant if the skin is shiny and tight.
- ♥ The eggplant will want to stick a bit to the pan, even with a nice coating of oil, so use a flexible spatula when stirring and be sure to scrape the bottom of the pan often.

> 2 large eggplants (about 3 pounds)
> 2 tablespoons canola oil or peanut oil
> 1 cup sliced red onion
> ¼ teaspoon salt
> 2 tablespoons minced or crushed garlic
> 3 to 4 serrano chiles, in thin strips or rounds
> ⅓ cup dry sherry
> 2 to 3 tablespoons (packed) brown sugar
> 2 tablespoons soy sauce
> 2 tablespoons fresh lime juice
> 1 cup (packed) fresh mint leaves, coarsely chopped

1) Cut the eggplants lengthwise into ½-inch-thick slices, then crosswise into ½-inch-thick sticks.

2) Place a large, deep skillet or wok over medium heat. After about a minute, add the oil and swirl to coat the pan. Add the onion, eggplant, and salt, and cook, stirring, for about 5 minutes.

3) Add the garlic, chiles, and sherry, and continue cooking and stirring another 5 minutes.

4) In a small bowl, combine the sugar, soy sauce, and lime juice with ¼ cup water and stir until the sugar dissolves. Stir this into the eggplant, then cover the pan, turn the heat to low, and cook, stirring frequently, for another 10 minutes, or until the eggplant is very tender and has collapsed in volume by about half. (If the eggplant seems to be browning more quickly than it is becoming tender, add a splash of water.)

5) Remove from heat, stir in the mint, and serve immediately.

~ Yield: 4 to 5 servings ~

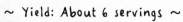

Grilled, Filled Endive
with
Cranberry-Speckled Green Rice

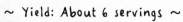

Belgian endive just begs to be stuffed! And usually this is a chilled, salad-y affair. Here's an idea for autumn or winter: Fill those perfect little boat-shaped leaves with rice and grill them briefly in olive oil to serve as a warm side dish. Grilling the endive brings out a slight (and very pleasant) bitterness that is balanced by the cranberries.

NOTE:
♥   You can make the rice (page 91) up to a day ahead and store it in a tightly covered container in the refrigerator. Heat it gently in a microwave or a 300°F oven before stuffing the endive leaves.

> 3/4 cup dried cranberries
> 1 recipe Very Green Rice (page 91), still warm or reheated
> 20 crisp leaves Belgian endive (5 to 6 tight heads)
> 1 to 2 tablespoons extra-virgin olive oil

1) Add the cranberries to the warm rice and mix well.

2) Place up to 4 tablespoons rice into the cavity of each endive leaf, lightly pressing and molding the filling into place. It will be a slightly delicate process.

3) Place a large skillet over medium heat. After about a minute, add the olive oil and swirl to coat the pan.

4) Gently place the filled endives in the skillet, placing them rice-side up and with the sides touching, so they can prop one another up. Cover the pan and let them heat through for just a few minutes. When done to your liking, use tongs or a spatula to remove them from the pan. Serve right away.

~ Yield: About 6 servings ~

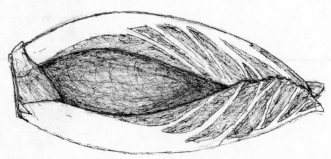

Self-Braised Escarole
with
Garlic & Golden Raisins

Escarole is a delicate, curly chicory that lives on the border between the salad bowl and the sauté pan. We're cooking it this time, and the result is a lovely bittersweet mouthful that goes well with just about anything.

NOTES:
- ♥ This cooks down a lot! You'll start out with a bushy panful, and it will reduce greatly.
- ♥ The optional butter goes a long way for flavor.

> 2 medium-sized heads escarole (about 10 ounces each)
> 1 tablespoon extra-virgin olive oil
> 1 teaspoon unsalted butter (optional)
> 1 teaspoon minced or crushed garlic
> Salt, to taste
> 1 to 2 tablespoons golden raisins

1) Trim the bottom ⅛ inch from the base of the escarole, then separate the leaves, wash them in cold water, and spin dry in a salad spinner. Coarsely chop and set aside.

2) Place a large, deep skillet over medium heat. After about a minute, add the olive oil and swirl to coat the pan. Melt in the butter if desired, then stir in the garlic.

3) Add the escarole, and sprinkle lightly with salt. Turn with tongs a few times, then cover (pressing it to fit, if necessary, over the bulky leaves) and cook for about 5 minutes. Turn a few more times, replace the cover, and cook until the escarole wilts to about half its initial volume.

4) Stir in the raisins and cook uncovered for another 5 to 10 minutes or so, turning frequently with tongs, until most of the liquid has evaporated. (Escarole gives off a lot of juices as it cooks, thus the "self-braising" title.) Serve hot, warm, or at room temperature.

~ Yield: 4 servings ~

Sautéed Fennel with Crispy Fried Lemon

Is it a snack or a side dish? I don't know, because I have trouble getting it to the table before eating it all myself.

NOTE:

♥ Use Meyer lemons, if you can get some. They are expensive (unless you live in California and grow your own), but you only need one or two. The special perfume and flavor of Meyers are magical, making them well worth seeking out at a specialty or farmers market. That said, if you can't find them, regular lemons will do just fine.

> 2 large fennel bulbs
> Extra-virgin olive oil
> ½ cup unbleached all-purpose flour
> ⅛ teaspoon salt
> Freshly ground black pepper, to taste
> 1 large lemon or 2 smaller ones

1) Use a very sharp knife to remove the stalks, stems, and fronds—and to trim the tough root end from the fennel. Cut the bulbs into ⅛- to ¼-inch-thick slices. From there, cut the slices into thin batons.

2) Preheat the oven to 275°F. Place a large, deep skillet over medium heat. After about a minute, add some olive oil and swirl to coat the pan. Add the fennel batons and sauté, stirring often, for 8 to 10 minutes, or until golden brown and tender to your liking. Transfer to an ovenproof serving platter and keep warm in the preheated oven while you prepare the lemon slices.

3) In a small, shallow bowl, combine the flour, salt, and a few grinds of pepper.

4) Use a very sharp knife or a mandoline to slice the lemon(s) paper-thin.

5) Return the skillet to the stove, this time to medium-high heat. Pour in enough olive oil to make a pool ⅛ inch deep.

6) While the oil is heating, drag the lemon slices through the flour mixture on one side, then back on the other, shaking off any excess, as you'll you want a very thin coating.

7) When the oil is hot enough to sizzle a bread crumb, slide each coated lemon slice into the hot oil, fitting in as many slices as you can without their overlapping. Cook until golden brown, about 1 minute, but watch carefully, as they can go from brown to burned in seconds. Use tongs or a slotted spoon to carefully turn the slices over in the hot oil and continue to cook until the second side is golden brown, about 1 minute longer.

8) Carefully transfer the lemon slices to a paper towel-lined plate. (If you couldn't fit all the slices in the oil at once, dust the remaining slices with the flour mixture and fry as above.)

9) Place the crispy lemon slices in a border around the sautéed fennel and serve.

~ Yield: 4 servings ~

fennel
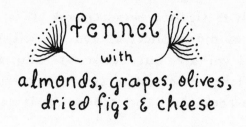

with
almonds, grapes, olives,
dried figs & cheese

A perfect summer lunch — or a palate-cleansing course before or after dinner.

NOTES:
- ♥ Use a very sharp knife or a mandoline to slice the fennel paper-thin.
- ♥ Make this about an hour before you intend to serve it.

> 2 medium fennel bulbs, very thinly sliced (about 2 cups)
> 1½ cups red seedless grapes, cut in half
> About 15 oil-cured or kalamata olives, pitted and sliced
> 5 or 6 dried figs, cut into small pieces
> 2 to 3 tablespoons extra-virgin olive oil and/or roasted almond oil
> 1 tablespoon fresh lemon juice (or to taste)
> Salt, to taste
> Freshly ground black pepper, to taste
> ½ cup blanched, slivered almonds, lightly toasted
> A small piece of hard cheese (Parmigiano-Reggiano, pecorino, or Asiago),
> shaved into thin slices with a vegetable peeler

1) In a medium-sized bowl, toss together the fennel, grapes, olives, and figs.

2) Drizzle in the olive oil (and/or roasted almond oil) and lemon juice, and toss until everything is lightly but thoroughly coated. Sprinkle lightly with salt and pepper, and toss again. Taste to adjust the lemon juice, then cover and refrigerate until serving (but not longer than about 1 hour).

3) Just before serving, drizzle in some more fresh lemon juice to taste (about 1 tablespoon is my taste) and sprinkle in the almonds and cheese shavings. Toss quickly but thoroughly, and serve right away.

~ Yield: 4 servings ~

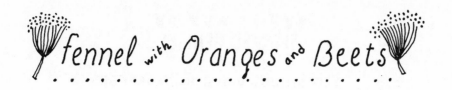

fennel with Oranges and Beets

Colorful and refreshing, this is a perfect first course (or lunch) for autumn.

NOTES:
- ♥ You can cook the beets any way you prefer — by steaming, boiling, or roasting. (Roasting instructions are on page 15.)
- ♥ Use a very sharp knife or a mandoline to slice the fennel paper-thin.
- ♥ The oranges and beets can be prepared up to 2 days ahead. In fact, it's preferable to do the oranges ahead, so they can give off a lot of juice.

6 oranges
1 pound beets, cooked until tender, then peeled and thinly sliced
1 to 2 tablespoons extra-virgin olive oil or roasted walnut oil
3 tablespoons raspberry vinegar or cider vinegar
Salt (optional)
½ teaspoon minced or crushed garlic
1 medium fennel bulb, very thinly sliced (about 2 cups)
Finely minced fennel fronds, for garnish

1) Cut the peel from the oranges, then section them over a bowl to catch all the juice. (To section an orange, just cut with a sawing motion up and down the membranes to release the sections. Squeeze the remaining juice into the bowl and discard the membranes.)

2) Place the beets in a medium-sized bowl and add the olive oil, vinegar, a few dashes of salt (if desired), garlic, and orange sections with all their juice. Stir until well combined.

3) Add the sliced fennel and stir again. Cover tightly and let marinate at room temperature (or in the refrigerator if the kitchen is hot) for a minimum of 2 hours and for as long as a day.

4) Serve cold or at room temperature, topped with a light sprinkling of the minced fennel fronds.

~ Yield: 6 servings ~

SHAVED FENNEL
WITH
RED ONION, OLIVE OIL, & ORANGES

Simple and seriously refreshing, this dish can be served as an appetizer, side dish, salad, or palate cleanser. I actually like it for dessert, but that's probably just me. Whatever its placement in your meal, be sure to serve it cold.

NOTES:
- ♥ Use a mandoline on its thinnest adjustment to prepare the fennel and onions. If you don't have a mandoline, cut the vegetables as thin as you possibly can with a very sharp knife.
- ♥ If you cover this tightly and refrigerate it, it will keep surprisingly well for up to 2 days.

> 1 large fennel bulb, shaved (4 to 5 cups)
> ½ medium red onion, shaved (about ½ cup)
> 5 tablespoons extra-virgin olive oil
> ⅛ teaspoon salt (or to taste)
> 3 oranges—peeled, seeded, and sectioned
> A handful of fronds from the fennel, snipped into tiny pieces
>   with scissors
> Freshly ground black pepper, to taste

1) Combine the shaved fennel, red onion, olive oil, and salt in a medium-sized bowl and toss with a fork.

2) Add the oranges, and stir gently. Cover and chill until cold (unless the ingredients were very cold to begin with).

3) Just before serving, toss in the snipped, feathery fronds from the fennel. Top each serving with a few grinds of black pepper.

~ Yield: 4 to 5 servings ~

⸪ BRIGHT GREENS ⸪
on a bed of
～ Creamy Polenta ～

Consider using some of the more elusive, serious greens, such as dandelion, mustard, kohlrabi, or kale.

NOTES:

♥ Use small leaves if you can get them. This way you can probably avoid having to stem them, and the only chopping necessary will be to cut them in half or so. However, if you can only get larger greens and they have considerable stalks, remove and discard the stalks and chop the leaves into bite-sized pieces.

♥ Sauté the greens (they are very quick!) during the last couple minutes of cooking the polenta, so you can serve them together, fresh from the stove.

♥ Polenta will keep for several days in a tightly covered container in the refrigerator. Reheat in a microwave or by mashing it in a bowl and possibly adding a little hot milk.

> 4 cups water
> Salt, to taste
> 1 cup polenta (coarse cornmeal)
> Up to 1 cup grated cheese (fontina, sharp cheddar, or Parmesan)
> 2 tablespoons extra-virgin olive oil
> 5 to 8 cups (packed) small greens (about ¾ pound) — stemmed and chopped, as necessary
> 1 teaspoon minced or crushed garlic

1) Pour 3 cups water into a medium-sized saucepan. Add about ½ teaspoon salt and bring to a boil. Meanwhile, place the polenta in a bowl with 1 cup cold or room-temperature water and stir until it is completely moistened.

2) When the water boils, turn down the heat to a simmer and spoon in the wet polenta. It will blend in instantly. Cook over medium-low heat, stirring slowly and often with a wooden spoon, until it turns creamy-thick (about 20 minutes). Remove from heat, stir in the cheese, and add salt to taste, if desired.

3) Place a large, deep skillet over medium heat. After about a minute, add the oil and swirl to coat the pan. Toss in the greens and a dash or two of salt, turn the heat up to medium-high, and stir-fry, turning with tongs, for about 30 seconds. Sprinkle in the garlic and cook, turning with tongs, for another minute or so, until just slightly wilted and very bright green. Divide polenta and place the freshly cooked greens on top. Serve immediately.

～ Yield: 4 to 5 servings ～

DRY·SAUTÉED
BRAISING GREENS
with LAYERS of GARLIC

Here's your chance to experience those intriguing "braising greens" often found next to the bulk salad mix and spinach in better produce departments and farmers markets.

NOTES:
- ♥ "Braising greens" often contain miniature specimens of a greater assortment of leaves than you might otherwise purchase by the bunch (or at all). Dandelion greens, baby red mustard, tatsoi, tiny kale, diminutive beet greens, and so on are often found in these mixes. Make sure they are perky and not at all wilted, and cook them within a day of purchasing. They lose their spark if they sit around.
- ♥ Roasted garlic has a handsomely bitter flavor that is both deeper and milder than fresh garlic. Roasted and fresh team up really well together to embrace an assortment of greens.
- ♥ Roast the garlic as much as several days ahead of time. Store it in a sealed plastic bag in the refrigerator until use.
- ♥ Make this in 2 batches, so the pan won't be crowded. Leaf contact with the hot pan is key.

> 3 tablespoons extra-virgin olive oil (plus extra, if desired)
> 2 medium-sized bulbs garlic
> 8 to 10 cups (packed) braising greens (about a pound)
> ½ to 1 teaspoon minced or crushed garlic
> Salt, to taste

1) Preheat the oven to 375°F. Line a small baking tray with foil and use a ½ teaspoon measure to make 2 small pools of olive oil.

2) Stand the garlic bulbs root-side down on the prepared tray, and roast for 35 to 40 minutes, or until they feel soft when gently squeezed. Remove the tray from the oven and let the bulbs cool until comfortable to handle. Separate the cloves and squeeze each one over a small bowl, releasing the pulp. (Some cloves might keep their shape, while others turn to mush. All forms are welcome.)

You can also peel all the garlic while it is still uncooked and wrap the cloves in a tight little foil packet, spooning in about a teaspoon of olive oil. Roast the packet for about 20 to 30 minutes at 325°F, or until the cloves are very soft.

3) Stem the greens, if necessary. Leave them whole if very small or coarsely chop if medium-small. (Your call.)

4) Place a large, deep skillet over medium heat. After about a minute, add half the remaining olive oil and swirl to coat the pan. Toss in half of the greens, turn the heat up to medium-high, and stir-fry, turning with tongs, for about 5 minutes, or until wilted. Stir in half the fresh garlic, sprinkle lightly with salt, if desired, then transfer to a medium-sized bowl, and set aside.

5) Repeat step 4 with the remaining olive oil and greens. When the leaves have wilted and the fresh garlic is mixed in, reduce the heat to medium low, and return the first batch of greens to the pan. Add the roasted garlic, turning everything together with tongs to combine. Add a little extra olive oil, if desired, and taste to adjust the salt. Serve hot, warm, or at room temperature.

~ Yield: 4 to 5 servings ~

BITTER GREENS
WITH
SWEET ONIONS AND SOUR CHERRIES

I love the taste of sour or tart fruit in savory dishes—especially in this one, where the flavors of the greens, onions, and cherries are all equally strong. The result is surprisingly balanced and smooth.

NOTES:

♥ I like to use a mixture of collards, beet greens, dandelion, and kale. The amount of greens below might seem enormous, but don't forget they will cook way down.

♥ Vidalia onions are terrific, but if you can't find them, just use regular ones.

♥ This dish gives off a lot of cooking liquid, but it is too pretty and delicious to let evaporate. So just include some with each serving, especially if you are pairing this dish with pasta or rice.

> 1 tablespoon extra-virgin olive oil
> 2 cups sliced onions (a sweet variety, such as Vidalia, if available)
> 3 large bunches fresh greens, stemmed if necessary, and coarsely chopped (about 12 cups)
> Salt, to taste
> 1 cup fresh sour cherries, pitted (or canned unsweetened sour cherries, drained— or dried sour cherries)
> Freshly ground black pepper, to taste

1) Place a large, deep skillet over medium heat. After about a minute, add the olive oil and swirl to coat the pan. Add the onions and sauté over high heat for about 5 minutes. Reduce the heat to medium, cover the pan, and let the onions cook until very tender, about 10 more minutes.

2) Add the greens in batches, sprinkling very lightly with salt after each addition, and turning them with tongs, bringing up the wilted ones from the bottom to the top of the pile.

3) When all the greens have wilted, stir in the cherries and cook for just about 2 minutes longer (less, if using dried cherries).

4) Transfer to a platter and grind on a generous amount of black pepper. Serve hot or warm.

~ Yield: 4 to 6 servings ~

BITTER GREENS
WITH
SWEET ONIONS AND TART CHEESE

A variation on the preceding recipe, this version contains more onions and substitutes feta cheese for the sour cherries. Superb on any short, substantial pasta, it also tastes good by itself, with a big chunk of crusty bread to mop up the juices.

NOTE:
- ♥ I recommend a combination of kale, escarole or chard, and mustard greens to collaborate with the pungent flavor of the cheese.

> 2 tablespoons extra-virgin olive oil
> 3 cups sliced onions (a sweet variety, such as Vidalia, if available)
> 3 large bunches fresh greens, stemmed if necessary, and coarsely chopped (about 12 cups)
> Salt, to taste
> Up to 1 cup feta cheese or ricotta salata, crumbled
> Freshly ground black pepper, to taste

1) Place a large, deep skillet over medium heat. After about a minute, add the olive oil and swirl to coat the pan. Add the onions and sauté over high heat for about 5 minutes. Reduce the heat to medium, cover the pan, and let the onions cook until very tender, about 10 more minutes.

2) Add the greens in batches, sprinkling very lightly with salt after each addition and turning them with tongs, bringing up the wilted ones from the bottom to the top of the pile.

3) When all the greens have wilted, stir in the cheese and cook for just about 2 minutes longer.

4) Transfer to a platter and grind on a generous amount of black pepper. Serve hot or warm, on or next to pasta or grains, or by itself.

~ Yield: 4 to 6 servings ~

//////// *Best Ever!* ////////
Green Beans Amandine
〉〉〉〉〉〉〉〉〉〉〉〉〉〉〉〉〉〉

The classic preparation, only better.

NOTE:

♥ This tastes even better when topped with Leek "Chips" (page 73), so I recommend that you plan to make some ahead of time.

> 1 tablespoon extra-virgin olive oil
> 2 teaspoons unsalted butter
> 3/4 cup chopped almonds
> 1 teaspoon minced or crushed garlic
> 1½ pounds green beans
> ¼ teaspoon salt
> Leek "Chips" (page 73), for garnish (optional)

1) Put up a large saucepan of water to boil.

2) In the meantime, place a large, deep skillet over medium heat. After about a minute, add the olive oil, melt in the butter, and swirl to coat the pan. Turn the heat down to low, add the almonds, and cook, stirring frequently, for about 5 to 8 minutes, or until the almonds give off a toasty aroma. During the last couple of minutes, stir in the garlic. (Be careful not to let any of it burn.) Remove from the heat, and set aside.

3) Meanwhile, when the water from step 1 boils, turn the heat down to low and add the green beans. Simmer for 3 to 5 minutes, or until the beans turn bright green and shiny and are beginning to become tender. (This is imprecise.) Dump the green beans into a colander in the sink and drain thoroughly.

4) Return the pan of almonds to the stove over medium-low heat. Add the green beans, turning them with tongs until they become completely coated (or at least well mingled) with the almonds. Sprinkle in the salt as you go. Serve hot, warm, or at room temperature, topped with the leek "chips," if desired.

~ Yield: 4 to 5 servings ~

GREEN BEANS
with Crunchy Peanut-Lemon Coating

The fresher and firmer the green beans, the better this will taste.

1 to 1½ cups peanuts (unsalted or lightly salted)
2 tablespoons canola or peanut oil
2 tablespoons minced fresh ginger
½ teaspoon grated lemon zest
1 tablespoon minced garlic
¼ teaspoon salt (possibly more, if the peanuts are salted)
1 pound fresh green beans, trimmed and cut into 1½-inch pieces
Red pepper flakes, to taste
1 tablespoon fresh lemon juice

1) Place the peanuts in a blender and grind briefly until they form a coarse meal. Set aside.

2) Place a large, deep skillet over medium heat. After about a minute, add 1 tablespoon of the oil and swirl to coat the pan. Add the ginger and sauté for a few minutes, then add the crushed peanuts, plus the lemon zest and garlic. Cook over medium-low heat for about 10 minutes, stirring often, until the peanuts are lightly toasted. Transfer this mixture to a medium-large bowl, and if the peanuts are unsalted, stir in some salt to taste. Set aside.

3) Wipe out the pan with a paper towel, then return it to the stove over medium heat. Wait about a minute, then add another tablespoon of oil and swirl to coat the pan. Turn up the heat, add the green beans, and stir-fry over high heat for about 5 minutes. Somewhere along the way, sprinkle with about ¼ teaspoon salt and a big pinch of red pepper flakes.

4) Stir-fry just a few minutes longer, or until the beans are divinely tender-crisp. Add the peanut mixture and the lemon juice, tossing everything together. Taste to adjust the salt and red pepper flakes, if necessary, and serve right away.

~ Yield: 4 to 5 servings ~

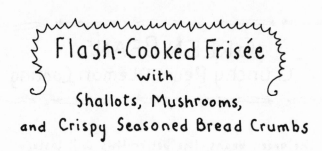

Flash-Cooked Frisée
with
Shallots, Mushrooms,
and Crispy Seasoned Bread Crumbs

Frisée, a standard component of salad mixes, also comes in individual heads that can be used for salad or cooked—with delightful results. For some reason, heads of this pale-green, curly chicory are usually either tiny or jumbo—it's hard to find anything in between. So it's best to go by weight. The amount below translates to about 8 cups of lightly packed greens before sautéing.

NOTE:
♥ Make the Crispy Seasoned Bread Crumbs well ahead of time.

> 1½ tablespoons extra-virgin olive oil
> ¼ cup minced shallots
> ⅛ teaspoon salt (or to taste)
> ½ pound mushrooms, wiped clean, stemmed, and sliced
> ¾ pound frisée (about 3 small heads), core removed and
>   leaves chopped into 2-inch lengths
> Freshly ground black pepper, to taste
> ¼ cup Crispy Seasoned Bread Crumbs (recipe follows)
> Fresh lemon wedges, for garnish

1) Place a large skillet over medium heat. After about a minute, add the olive oil and swirl to coat the pan. Add the shallots and salt; cook for about a minute.

2) Add the mushrooms and continue cooking, stirring often, for about 5 minutes, or until the shallots and mushrooms turn a light golden brown.

3) Add the frisée and cook, tossing once or twice, for about 2 minutes, or until most of the frisée is wilted. Season to taste with additional salt and some freshly ground black pepper.

4) Serve hot, warm, or at room temperature, topped with the bread crumbs and garnished with fresh lemon wedges.

~ Yield: 4 servings ~

Crispy Seasoned Bread Crumbs

These are especially tasty when made with day-old sourdough bread—but any sturdy bread will do. You can keep these "fresh" bread crumbs in an airtight container in the refrigerator or a zip-style plastic bag in the freezer. This recipe makes about 1 cup of bread crumbs.

3 ounces sturdy bread (preferably sourdough)
1 tablespoon extra-virgin olive oil
Salt, to taste
Freshly ground black pepper, to taste

1) Trim and discard any crust that has gone completely hard, then tear the remaining bread into 1-inch pieces. Transfer to a food processor and pulse a few times until you have crumbs of your preferred size.

2) Place a medium-sized skillet over medium heat. After about a minute, add the olive oil and swirl to coat the pan. Add the bread crumbs and cook, stirring constantly, until the crumbs are crispy and a deep golden brown. (This takes anywhere from 5 to 10 minutes, on average.)

3) Transfer to a small bowl and season to taste with salt and freshly ground black pepper.

Dramatically Seared GREEN BEANS

Once the beans are trimmed, all you need is a large hot pan, and the rest is one big, quick sizzling action!

NOTE:
- ♥ These will keep for up to a week in a tightly covered container (or a zip-style plastic bag) in the refrigerator.

> 2 tablespoons canola or peanut oil
> 1 pound whole green beans, trimmed
> Salt, to taste
> 1 tablespoon minced or crushed garlic
> Red pepper flakes, to taste

1) Place a large, deep skillet or wok over medium heat. After about 2 minutes, add the oil and swirl to coat the pan.

2) Turn the heat to high and wait another 30 seconds or so, then add the green beans and a big pinch of salt.

3) Cook over high heat, shaking the pan and/or using tongs to turn and move the beans so they cook quickly and evenly.

4) After about 3 minutes, taste to see if the beans are done to your liking. They should be relatively crunchy, but you get to decide. If you like them cooked a little more, keep going until they're your kind of tender.

5) Sprinkle in the garlic and some red pepper flakes, and cook for just a minute longer. Serve hot, warm, or at room temperature.

~ Yield: 4 to 6 servings ~

ⱽⱽⱽⱽⱽⱽ ⱽⱽ ⱽⱽⱽⱽ
LEEK CHIPS
ⱽⱽⱽⱽⱽⱽⱽⱽⱽⱽ

Leek rings are dried out and crispened in the oven—reminiscent, in a loose way, of those French-fried onion rings retro cooks used to decorate green bean casseroles. Only better! These are addictive as a snack or nibble with cocktails—or as a topping to other dishes. You might need to make them often.

ⱽ ⱽ

NOTE:
♥ Store in a covered container at room temperature. They will keep for a week or longer, but taste best within a few hours of being made.

> 1 tablespoon extra-virgin olive oil
> 2 medium-sized leeks (1½-inch diameter)
> Salt, to taste
> Freshly ground black pepper, to taste

1) Preheat the oven to 250°F. Line a large baking tray with foil and coat with the oil.

2) Remove and discard the dark green leaves from the leeks. Slice off about ¼ inch from the root end as well. (You want the white and pale green portions only.) Use a very sharp knife to cut the leeks into ¼-inch slices, then transfer them to a large bowl of cold water. Use your fingers and thumb to separate the slices into rings, then swish the pieces around vigorously to remove any sand or grit that might be tucked in between the layers. With your hands or a large slotted spoon, lift the leek rings out of the water and transfer them to a colander in the sink. Drain thoroughly, then pat dry with a clean kitchen towel or paper towels.

3) Distribute the leek rings onto the prepared baking tray and toss to coat with the oil. Bake, stirring occasionally, until golden brown and crisp. (Note that some rings may be ready to remove at 30 minutes, others may take up to 60 minutes or longer—just remove them as they are done.)

4) Transfer the finished "chips" to a plate, season to taste with a few dashes of salt and pepper, and serve at room temperature.

ⱽ ⱽ

~ Yield: About 2 cups ~

Mushroom·Stuffed
MUSHROOMS
with Wild Rice and Goat Cheese

Here is the recipe for a mixed crowd of vegetarians and meat eaters. Everyone will be very happy! Vegetarians can make a complete meal out of one entire, generously (and deliciously) filled portobello, and the meat eaters can divide the mushrooms in half and share them for a very satisfying side dish.

NOTES:
- ♥ Cook a small batch of wild rice well ahead of time (½ cup rice cooked in 1¼ cups water for about an hour will yield more than enough for this recipe).
- ♥ If you use a pan with an ovenproof handle, this can go directly from the stove to the broiler.
- ♥ You can assemble the mushrooms (through step 4) up to 2 days ahead of time and refrigerate them, wrapped individually and tightly in plastic wrap.

2 tablespoons extra-virgin olive oil
1 cup minced onion
6 ounces domestic mushrooms, cleaned, stemmed, and minced
1 teaspoon minced or crushed garlic
¼ teaspoon salt
1 packed cup cooked wild rice
2 ounces herbed goat cheese
Freshly ground black pepper to taste
4 portobello mushrooms (4-inch-diameter)
Juice from half a lemon
A handful of cherry tomatoes, halved
4 teaspoons fine bread crumbs
Freshly minced or torn flat-leaf parsley, for garnish

1) Place a large, deep skillet over medium heat. After about a minute, add 1 tablespoon of oil, and swirl to coat the pan. Add the onion and cook, stirring often, for 5 minutes or until the onion becomes translucent.

2) Add the domestic mushrooms, garlic, and salt, and cook uncovered for 8 to 10 minutes, stirring frequently, until the mushrooms are soft and most of the liquid they have expressed is evaporated. Stir in the wild rice, and cook for just a minute or two longer.

3) Transfer the mixture to a medium-large bowl and crumble or fork in the goat cheese. Stir it in as it melts, so it gets distributed as evenly as possible. Set the bowl aside.

4) Remove and discard the portobello mushroom stems, and peel the mushrooms, if necessary. Use a spoon to scrape out and discard the soft gills from the inside of the mushroom caps. Divide the filling evenly among the hollowed-out mushrooms. You will have approximately ⅓ cup of filling for each mushroom. Sprinkle with lemon juice, and arrange the tomato halves cut-side up over the tops.

5) Wipe out the skillet with a paper towel, and return it to the stove. Turn the heat to medium, and add the remaining tablespoon of oil. Place the filled mushrooms in the pan, cover, and cook undisturbed for about 10 to 15 minutes, or until the mushrooms are cooked through. (You might need to use two pans, or do this in two batches.)

6) Preheat the broiler. Sprinkle the top of each mushroom with 1 teaspoon of fine bread crumbs and broil for 3 to 5 minutes, or until the top is golden. (Watch it carefully, so it doesn't burn!)

7) Serve hot, warm, or at room temperature—whole or cut in half (depending on what you are serving this with)—and topped with a scattering of minced or torn parsley.

~ Yield: 4 or more servings ~

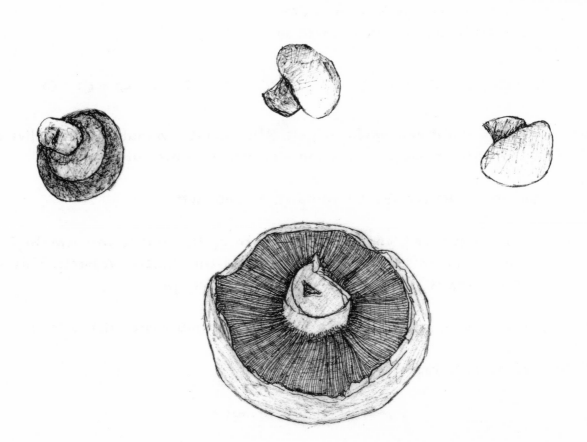

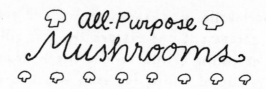

All-Purpose Mushrooms

Sautéed mushrooms fit perfectly in many contexts, and here is *the* recipe. Use these mushrooms for omelets or as a topping for any grilled tofu, tempeh, chicken, or fish. Or just pile them on a piece of toast. Divine!

NOTES:

♥ For deeper flavor, use a combination of domestic and wild mushrooms (shiitakes, chanterelles, oyster mushrooms, morels) if available. The proportions should be about half domestic and half wild mushrooms.

♥ This stores and reheats well. It should last for about a week in the refrigerator if kept in a tightly covered container. Reheat in the microwave or over very low heat on the stovetop.

♥ The optional butter goes a long way for flavor.

> 1 tablespoon extra-virgin olive oil
> About 1 teaspoon unsalted butter (optional)
> 1 cup minced onion
> 4 heaping cups mushrooms (1 pound), sliced or minced
> ½ teaspoon salt (possibly more)
> ½ teaspoon dried thyme
> 1 tablespoon fresh lemon juice
> Freshly ground black pepper, to taste

1) Place a large, deep skillet over medium heat. After about a minute, add the olive oil and swirl to coat the pan. If you like, you can also melt in some butter.

2) Add the onion and sauté for about 8 minutes, or until soft.

3) Stir in the mushrooms, salt, and thyme, and turn up the heat to medium-high. Sauté until the mushrooms are cooked through and their juices evaporate. This should only take a few minutes if the pan is hot and large enough.

4) Toss in the lemon juice, and add black pepper (and possibly more salt) to taste.

5) Serve hot, warm, or at room temperature.

~ Yield: About 4 servings ~

Caramelized Onion-
Orange
MARMALADE

Serve this sparkling, sweet-sour condiment with any green vegetable or grilled tofu, tempeh, chicken, or fish. It's also good with scrambled eggs, spread on toast, or as a topping for your favorite cheese.

NOTE:
- ❤ Zest the oranges before squeezing the juice. (You will likely need more than 1 orange to get enough zest.) A nice method for this dish is to shave the zest from the orange with a sturdy vegetable peeler, and then chop it coarsely with a sharp knife.

> 1 tablespoon canola oil or peanut oil
> 4 cups minced onion (any kind)
> ½ teaspoon salt
> 1 tablespoon balsamic vinegar
> 3 tablespoons fresh orange juice
> 1 tablespoon light-colored honey
> 1 to 2 tablespoons chopped orange zest

1) Place a medium-sized skillet over medium heat and wait about 2 minutes. Add the oil and swirl to coat the pan. Add the onions, and sauté them for about 5 minutes, or until they are soft and translucent. Turn the heat to low, and cover the pan.

2) Cook, covered, for 15 minutes, stirring occasionally. After 15 minutes, stir in the vinegar, then cover, and cook for another 5 minutes. Stir in the orange juice and honey, and cook, uncovered, for about 5 minutes longer.

3) Remove from the heat, and stir in the orange zest. Cool to room temperature, then pack into a jar with a tight-fitting lid. Cover and refrigerate for up to 3 weeks. Use it on or with any savory dish.

~ Yield: 1 cup ~

Mollie's Quite Surprising MASHED PARSNIPS

Parsnips are out there, just waiting for you to discover them. Here's a good way to do that. I guarantee that you will be Quite Surprised by their subtle sweetness.

NOTES:

♥ Parsnips come in many sizes. Try to get small or medium ones (up to 8 inches long) as the giant ones tend to have a tough inner core that doesn't soften up too well.

♥ This will keep for up to 5 days in a tightly covered container in the refrigerator. It reheats really well in a microwave.

> 2 pounds parsnips (about 6 medium ones, approximately 8 inches long, 2-inch diameter)
> 2 tablespoons extra-virgin olive oil
> 2 teaspoons balsamic vinegar (or to taste)
> ½ teaspoon salt (or to taste)
> Freshly ground black pepper, to taste

1) Put up a large saucepan of water to boil.

2) Meanwhile, peel the parsnips, and trim and discard the ends. Chop the parsnips into 2- to 3-inch pieces.

3) When the water boils, add the cut parsnips and cook them for about 10 minutes, or until very soft. Use a mesh scooper or a slotted spoon to remove them from the water, shaking out the excess, and transfer them to the work bowl of a food processor. (Remove the saucepan of water from the heat, but don't dump it out yet.)

4) Add the olive oil, vinegar, and salt to the parsnips, and process until very smooth. If they seem a bit dry, add a little of their cooking water. (If you don't have a food processor, just put everything in a bowl and mash well with a fork or a potato masher.)

5) Season to taste with black pepper (correcting the salt and vinegar along the way, if you so choose) and serve hot or warm.

~ Yield: 4 to 5 servings ~

GARLICKY PEA SHOOT TANGLE

Pea shoots can be eaten raw in salads or stir-fried very briefly in a hot pan. They have a good, strong flavor and a wonderful crunchy texture. Best of all, they require no chopping. Just rinse and drain them, and they're ready to dump in the pan.

NOTE:

♥ Roasted peanut oil has a deep flavor that greatly enhances this dish. Unlike other roasted nut oils, which are used mostly for "finishing," roasted peanut oil has a high smoke point and can be used for cooking. If you can't find it, use olive oil, and this will still taste great.

> 1 tablespoon roasted peanut oil or extra-virgin olive oil
> 1 pound pea shoots, rinsed, drained, and thoroughly dried
> 2 tablespoons minced or crushed garlic
> 1/4 teaspoon salt (or to taste)

1) Place a large, deep skillet or wok over medium heat. After about a minute, add the oil and swirl to coat the pan.

2) Add the pea shoots and garlic, and turn up the heat. Stir-fry for about 5 minutes, attempting to get the garlic distributed evenly through the tangle of shoots. Stir in the salt along the way. (It's easiest to use tongs or a large, long-handled fork for mixing.)

3) Remove from the heat as soon as the pea shoots are wilted and have turned deep green. Serve hot or warm.

~ Yield: 4 to 6 servings ~

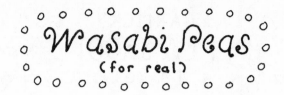

Wasabi Peas
(for real)

Snack food meets side dish, and the result is very difficult to stop eating. In this case, that is a good thing. This won't be hit-over-the-head spicy, just nice.

NOTES:
- ♥ Defrost the peas by placing them in a colander in a sink and running them under lukewarm water. Drain well before proceeding.
- ♥ You can find wasabi paste (usually sold in tubes) in Asian groceries or in the imported foods section of your supermarket. Wasabi also comes in powdered form, which can easily be made into paste by adding water. (Follow the instructions on the container.)
- ♥ For best results, make this about 15 minutes before serving, so the peas have time to absorb the flavors of the onion and wasabi.

1 to 2 teaspoons unsalted butter
1 cup minced onion
1 pound green peas (frozen and defrosted)
Salt to taste
2 to 3 tablespoons wasabi paste (possibly a little more)
1 tablespoon extra-virgin olive oil
3 tablespoons water (possibly more)
Freshly ground black pepper to taste
Wasabi peas (the crunchy snack version) for the top (optional)

1) Melt the butter in a medium-sized skillet over medium heat. When it is melted, swirl to coat the pan.

2) Add the onion, and cook for 5 minutes over medium heat, stirring often. Add the peas and a few dashes of salt, and cook, shaking the pan from time to time, for 5 minutes longer.

3) Meanwhile, place the wasabi paste in a small bowl, and mash with the olive oil. Add water by the tablespoon until the mixture becomes a supple sauce, and pour this into the peas. Grind in some fresh black pepper as well. Stir gently (or just shake the pan to keep the peas from breaking) as you incorporate the sauce. Turn the heat to low, cover the pan, and cook for 10 minutes.

4) Transfer to a serving bowl, and let it sit for 15 minutes so the flavors can meld. Serve warm or at room temperature—plain or topped with a sprinkling of wasabi snack peas for extra crunch and heat.

~ Yield: 4 to 5 servings ~

❧ ROASTED RED PEPPERS ❧
with GARLIC & LIME

Serve this as a topping for crostini (superb on top of goat cheese!) or fresh bread—or as a relish on top of grilled tofu, chicken, or fish. It also makes a lovely appetizer when accompanied by a platter of cheeses and olives.

NOTE:
♥ This recipe needs a minimum 4-hour marinating period. Thereafter, it keeps beautifully for up to a week if stored in a tightly covered container in the refrigerator. In fact, the flavor improves as it sits.

> ¼ cup extra-virgin olive oil
> 5 large red bell peppers
> 3 tablespoons fresh lime juice
> ¼ teaspoon salt (or to taste)
> 1 teaspoon minced or crushed garlic
> Freshly ground black pepper, to taste

1) Preheat the oven to 400°F. Line a baking tray with foil and coat with about 1 tablespoon of the olive oil.

2) Place the peppers on the tray, laying them on their sides. Roast in the center of the oven for about 30 to 35 minutes, turning the peppers with tongs every 5 to 8 minutes, so they will roast—and blister—fairly evenly.

3) When the peppers are quite soft and the skins have darkened and pulled away from the flesh, remove the tray from the oven. Use tongs to transfer the peppers to a bowl, then cover the bowl with a plate. Let the peppers cool until comfortable to handle. (The roasted peppers will express flavorful juices while cooling. Save this liquid and use it for soup stock or a sauce.)

4) Peel each pepper, using your hands and/or a paring knife. Also remove and discard the stems and seeds. Cut the peppers into small cubes or strips and transfer them to a second medium-sized bowl.

5) Add the remaining ingredients and mix gently. Cover tightly and refrigerate for at least 4 hours before serving. (Longer is fine.) Serve cold or at room temperature.

~ Yield: 4 servings ~

Nut-Crusted Portobello Fritters

Thin strips of meaty portobello mushrooms hold a crunchy nut coating very well, and make a wonderfully satisfying appetizer or side dish.

    4 medium (4-inch) portobello mushrooms
    1 cup almonds or hazelnuts
    ¼ cup grated Parmesan cheese
    ¼ teaspoon salt
    ⅛ teaspoon freshly ground black pepper
    3 large eggs
    2 to 3 tablespoons olive oil

    OPTIONAL:
    ♥ Arugula
    ♥ Capers
    ♥ Mayonnaise

1) Remove the mushroom stems and wipe the caps clean with a damp paper towel. Cut them into long slices about ½ inch thick, and set aside.

2) Place the nuts and cheese in a blender or food processor, and buzz in a few spurts or long pulses until the nuts are ground to the consistency of cornmeal. Transfer to a plate and stir in the salt and pepper.

3) Break the eggs into a pie pan and beat until smooth.

4) Dip both sides of each mushroom slice in the beaten egg, then press the wet surfaces firmly into the nut mixture. Transfer the coated mushrooms to another plate.

5) Place a large skillet over medium heat. After about a minute, add the olive oil and swirl to coat the pan. Arrange the coated mushroom slices in the pan. They can be touching but should not overlap. Sauté them for about 5 minutes on each side or until golden all over, then transfer them to a wire rack over a tray to cool. (Save any coating that might have fallen off. It's delicious!)

6) Serve hot, warm, or at room temperature—plain or on a bed of arugula leaves, sprinkled with a scattering of capers and a dollop of mayonnaise for dipping, if desired.

~ Yield: 4 to 6 servings (4 to 6 slices per serving) ~

PORTOBELLO PARMESAN

There are so many ways to fill a portobello! This one can be a light main course if served whole, or a substantial appetizer or side dish if cut in half.

NOTES:
- ♥ Assemble the ricotta mixture while the mushrooms are cooking.
- ♥ After you cut open the tomato, hold it over the sink and squeeze out the juice and seeds before slicing it.
- ♥ Use a skillet with an ovenproof handle so this can go directly from the stove to the broiler.
- ♥ Make this dish just before serving—it tastes best fresh from the broiler.

> 4 firm portobello mushrooms (4-inch-diameter)
> 1 tablespoon extra-virgin olive oil
> 3/4 cup ricotta cheese
> 1 teaspoon minced or crushed garlic
> 1/2 cup grated mozzarella cheese
> Freshly ground black pepper, to taste
> 1 medium-sized ripe-but-firm tomato, thinly sliced
> About 1 tablespoon thyme leaves (or about 1 teaspoon dried thyme)
> 3 tablespoons grated Parmesan cheese

1) Remove and discard the portobello stems, and scrape out and discard the gills, being careful not to damage the mushrooms' edges. (Okay to leave a few gills around the edges to protect them.)

2) Place a large skillet over medium heat. After about a minute, add the olive oil and swirl to coat the pan.

3) Lay the mushrooms cap-side down in the hot oil, and let them cook undisturbed for about 10 minutes. Turn them over and cook on the other side for 10 minutes, then flip them over one more time.

4) Meanwhile, combine the ricotta, garlic, and mozzarella in a small bowl, grinding in some black pepper, to taste. Add about 3 tablespoons of this filling to each mushroom cavity (okay to do this while they are still in the pan, if you can), spreading it gently into place.

5) Arrange a few tomato slices on each mound of cheese and sprinkle the tomatoes first with a little thyme, then with a nice coating of Parmesan. Heat the broiler.

6) Place the pan under the broiler for about 5 minutes or until the tops of the filled mushrooms turn a lovely shade of golden brown. (Watch carefully so they won't have a chance to burn, which can happen quickly!) Remove from the broiler and serve immediately.

~ Yield: 4 single or 8 shared servings ~

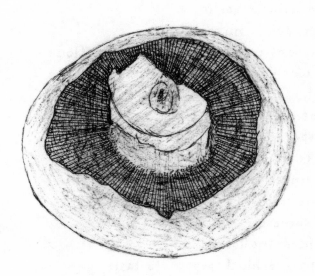

Potato, Turnip, & Carrot Gratin
with Garlic-Herb Béchamel Sauce

It's nice to slip in some turnips among the more familiar potatoes and carrots, for something slightly different.

NOTES:
- ♥ It's easiest to warm the milk in the microwave right in its measuring cup.
- ♥ Good bread crumbs are made by hand from good bread. My favorites for this recipe are either a home-style whole wheat or pumpernickel. Make your own bread crumbs by drying out some of your favorite bread, then crumbling it either by hand (in a plastic bag, so it won't go all over the place) or in a food processor with the steel blade (a few spurts).

> 2 tablespoons unsalted butter
> 1 teaspoon minced garlic
> ½ teaspoon dried thyme
> 1½ tablespoons unbleached all-purpose flour
> 1¼ cups warmed milk
> 1 bay leaf
> Salt, to taste
> White pepper, to taste
> Nonstick cooking spray
> ½ pound unpeeled Yukon gold potatoes
> ½ pound turnips
> ½ pound carrots
> 1 cup minced shallots
> Freshly ground black pepper, to taste
> 1 cup coarse bread crumbs
> ½ cup grated Swiss cheese (Gruyère or Emmenthaler)

1) Melt the butter in a small saucepan over low heat, adding the garlic and thyme when it is melted.

2) Whisk in the flour and keep whisking for a minute or so as it forms a thick paste.

3) Keep whisking as you drizzle in the warmed milk, keeping the mixture moving until there are no lumps.

4) Add the bay leaf and turn the heat way down. Cook, stirring frequently, for about 5 to 8 minutes, or until smooth and silky. Remove from the heat and remove the bay leaf. Stir in a dash of salt and a few shakes of white pepper, then set aside.

5) Preheat the oven to 375°F. Lightly spray a 2-quart gratin dish with nonstick spray.

6) Cut the potatoes, turnips, and carrots into very thin slices (about ⅛ inch). For the carrots, do this on the diagonal. Spread the cut vegetables (including the shallots) together in the prepared pan to make a single mixed layer. Sprinkle lightly with salt and black pepper.

7) Pour the béchamel sauce from step 4 over the top of the vegetables and cover the pan tightly with foil. Bake in the center of the oven for 1 hour, or until the vegetables are fork-tender. Remove the dish from the oven and remove the foil.

8) Heat the broiler. Sprinkle the bread crumbs and then the grated cheese on top of the vegetables. Broil until the cheese is melted and beginning to form a crust. Serve hot.

~ Yield: 4 to 5 servings ~

RADICCHIO·PORCINI
Risotto

The charm of any risotto, in addition to the flavor, is the textural contrast between the separate al dente grains and the thick, smooth sauce in which they are suspended. Ultra-comfort food!

NOTES:
- ♥ This will be even more delicious if you use a flavorful vegetable broth (such as Imagine brand) and a good, dry white wine that you would be happy drinking.
- ♥ It's possible to buy ¾ ounce of dried porcini mushrooms without having to sell your firstborn to afford it. Shop around (including on the Internet).
- ♥ Begin soaking the mushrooms about 45 minutes ahead of time.
- ♥ It is very important to serve risotto immediately after it is made, so the juxtaposed textures are maximized. (If it waits around or gets reheated, the rice will keep cooking and disappear into the background.)

¾ ounce dried porcini mushrooms
2 cups boiling water
4 cups vegetable broth
3 tablespoons extra-virgin olive oil
2 cups finely minced onion
1 tablespoon minced or crushed garlic
1½ cups arborio rice
¾ teaspoon salt (possibly more, to taste)
½ cup dry white wine, at room temperature
1 medium-sized (8-ounce) head radicchio, finely chopped (3 packed cups)
¾ cup grated Pecorino Romano or Parmesan cheese

1) Place the mushrooms in a medium-sized bowl and cover with the boiling water. Cover with a plate, and let stand for 30 minutes. Drain the mushrooms, squeezing out and saving all the water. Remove the stems, if necessary, and cut the mushrooms into thin strips.

2) Combine the mushroom water and the broth in a medium-large saucepan over medium heat. Bring to a boil, then lower the heat to a simmer.

3) Meanwhile, heat the oil in a 4-quart casserole over medium heat. Add the onion and sauté for 1 to 2 minutes, until softened.

4) Add the mushrooms, garlic, rice, and salt, and stir for 1 minute.

5) Pour in the wine and cook until it is all absorbed.

6) Stir in the radicchio, and then start to add the simmering broth ½ cup at a time, letting each addition be completely absorbed before adding another ½ cup. Reserve ¼ cup broth to be added at the end. It takes approximately 18 minutes to reach the al dente stage.

7) Stir in the remaining ¼ cup of broth and the cheese. Combine well and serve immediately.

~ Yield: 4 servings ~

Grilled Radicchio
with Touches of Fruit & Cheese

Grilled radicchio is perfect for those of us who love "bitter" as a flavor. And gorgonzola is the perfect complement to stand up to it. For more timid palates, the fontina takes the edge off a bit. And if radicchio is unavailable, red cabbage makes a lovely substitute — with either cheese.

NOTE:
♥ This dish is like a hot salad — the radicchio or cabbage is still a bit crunchy when done. But if you like a more tender mouthful, cook it a bit longer.

1 tablespoon extra-virgin olive oil
1 pound radicchio or red cabbage (or a combination), coarsely chopped
1 cup red seedless grapes, halved
¼ cup golden raisins
Up to 6 tablespoons crumbled gorgonzola or diced fontina
Salt and freshly ground black pepper, to taste

OPTIONAL TOPPINGS:
♥ 4 or more fresh, ripe figs, sliced or coarsely chopped
♥ Lightly toasted pine nuts

1) Place a large skillet over medium heat. After about a minute, add the olive oil and swirl to coat the pan. Add the radicchio, grapes, and raisins and cook, stirring often, until the radicchio is wilted and just tender, 3 to 4 minutes. (If using cabbage, you may want to cook it over medium heat for 5 minutes or so, for a softer result.)

2) Remove from the heat, add the cheese, and toss to combine. Season to taste with salt and freshly ground black pepper. Garnish with the fresh figs and toasted pine nuts, if desired. Serve hot, warm, or at room temperature.

~ Yield: 4 servings ~

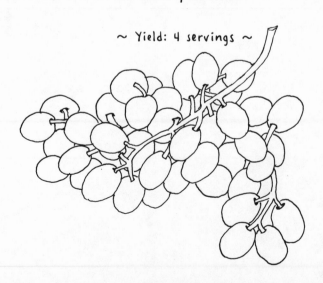

very green rice

Don't forget that herbs and all edible green leaves, no matter how small, are vegetables! And embedding them in rice is a very effective stealth delivery system. In this delicious recipe, the volume of minced herbs is equal to the amount of rice, and no one will know.

NOTE:
- ♥ This is a great way to use up leftover rice. If you need to cook it fresh, begin with 1½ cups uncooked long-grain brown rice and make it well ahead of time. It will yield 4½ cups cooked rice.

> 4 scallions, trimmed and cut into 2-inch lengths
> (whites and greens)
> 1 cup (loosely packed) each: watercress, flat-leaf parsley,
> mint leaves, and cilantro leaves
> 2 to 3 tablespoons extra-virgin olive oil
> 1 teaspoon minced or crushed garlic
> 4 to 5 cups cooked brown basmati rice
> ½ teaspoon salt (or to taste)
> ¾ cup lightly toasted pine nuts (optional)
> Squeezable wedges of lemon

1) Pile all the scallions and green herbs into the food processor and pulverize almost to a paste.

2) Place a large, deep skillet over medium heat. After about a minute, add the olive oil and swirl to coat the pan. Add the garlic and sauté by itself for just a minute, then add the processed herbs and cook, stirring, for about 5 minutes.

3) Add the rice, mixing it in with a fork until the green mixture is uniformly distributed. Stir in the salt and serve hot or warm, topped with pine nuts, if desired, and accompanied by a squeezable wedge of fresh lemon. Remind people to use it!

~ Yield: 4 to 6 servings ~

OVEN RATATOUILLE

In this (my favorite) version, everything gets roasted at a high temperature and then combined in the end. The flavors become very deep.

NOTES:
- ♥ Dried herbs added during the roasting process infuse the vegetables with even deeper flavor. Optional fresh herbs sprinkled on at serving time add another savory layer.
- ♥ Serve plain or on a bed of polenta and topped with a grilled "veggie" sausage and/or a freshly poached egg.

      3 to 4 tablespoons extra-virgin olive oil
      1 large globe eggplant (about 1 pound), cut into 3/4-inch cubes (peeling unnecessary if the skin is tight and smooth)
      2 pounds ripe plum tomatoes, cored
      6 medium-sized garlic cloves, unpeeled
      2 large bell peppers (red, yellow, or orange)
      2 cups coarsely chopped onion
      1 medium zucchini (7 to 8 inches long), cut into 1-inch cubes
      1½ teaspoons dried basil
      1 teaspoon dried marjoram or oregano
      ½ teaspoon each crumbled dried thyme and rosemary
      Salt and freshly ground black pepper, to taste

OPTIONAL TOPPINGS:
- ♥ Small amounts of fresh herbs (basil, marjoram or oregano, rosemary, thyme, and/or parsley)
- ♥ Pitted chopped olives

1) Arrange an oven rack in the topmost position, and another in the middle of the oven. Preheat the oven to 425°F. Line 1 small and 2 large baking trays with foil, and coat the foil generously with the olive oil.

2) Place the eggplant on one of the large trays, and toss to coat with the oil. Then push it to one side, keeping it in a single layer. Arrange the tomatoes on the other half of the tray, rolling them around so they get coated with oil. Wrap the garlic cloves (still in their skins) and a half teaspoon of water tightly in a piece of foil, and place this on the corner of the same tray.

3) Place the whole bell peppers on the small tray.

4) Spread the onions and the zucchini pieces on opposite ends of the remaining large tray, and toss to coat with the oil.

5) Place the eggplant tray on the middle shelf of the oven, and put the small sheet with the peppers on the upper rack. After 10 minutes, use tongs to turn everything over. Repeat this turning process after another 10 minutes or so. Gently squeeze the garlic to see if it is soft. If it is, remove it from the oven; if not, continue roasting.

6) Place the onion-zucchini tray on the middle shelf next to the one with the eggplant, and continue roasting all for another 10 minutes. Turn the peppers and tomatoes one more time, and toss the eggplant, onions, and zucchini to help them brown evenly. Sprinkle the eggplant, onions, and zucchini evenly with the dried herbs. Once again, squeeze the garlic to see if it is soft. If so, remove it from the oven; if not, continue roasting. Roast a final 10 minutes, or until the vegetables become deep golden brown and very tender.

7) Transfer the eggplant, onion, and zucchini to a large bowl. Let the peppers, tomatoes, and garlic sit for a few minutes, or until comfortable to handle. Peel the peppers, then chop the tomatoes and peeled peppers roughly into 1-inch pieces and add to the eggplant mixture. Slip the roasted garlic cloves from their skins, mash with a fork, and add to the eggplant mixture.

8) Toss until well combined. Season to taste with salt and freshly ground black pepper. Serve warm, at room temperature, or chilled—plain or topped with a sprinkling of freshly chopped herbs and/or olives.

~ Yield: 4 to 6 servings ~

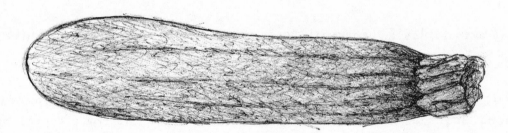

Roasted Root Vegetables
with PEAR GLAZE

Parsnips and rutabagas make a sunny quartet with the more familiar carrots and sweet potatoes, and the glaze adds sparkle.

NOTES:
- ♥ Look for smooth, taut skin on the root vegetables. (Skip the wrinkled ones that have begun to lose moisture.)
- ♥ Because you'll be roasting the vegetables in a baking dish or an equivalent pan, rather than on the usual foil-lined tray, you can add the glaze directly to the dish and bring the whole thing to the table. (I use a ceramic gratin oval.)
- ♥ Make the glaze while the vegetables roast. The glaze should be served hot or very warm, over warm or room-temperature vegetables.

> 1 to 2 tablespoons extra-virgin olive oil
> 3 to 4 medium carrots (about ¾ pound)
> 2 to 3 medium (8-inch) parsnips (about ¾ pound)
> 1 medium rutabaga (about ½ pound)
> 2 to 3 medium sweet potatoes (about ¾ pound)
> 1 cup pear nectar
> ¾ cup cider vinegar
> 2 tablespoons fresh lemon juice
> ⅓ cup light-colored honey
> Salt, to taste
> Freshly ground black pepper, to taste

1) Preheat the oven to 425°F. Generously coat a 2-quart baking dish with olive oil, and set aside.

2) Peel and cut all the vegetables into similar-sized pieces (½-inch-thick rounds or 1½-inch-long "logs" work best). Transfer the cut vegetables to the prepared baking dish, and toss to coat with the oil.

3) Place the dish in the center of the oven and roast the vegetables, stirring occasionally, for about 40 minutes, or until golden brown and fork-tender. When the vegetables are done to your liking, remove the dish from the oven.

4) In a shallow saucepan, combine the pear nectar, vinegar, lemon juice, and honey. Place the pan over medium heat and whisk to dissolve the honey. Bring the mixture to a boil, reduce the heat to maintain a steady simmer, and cook for 20 to 30 minutes, or until reduced to about ½ cup. (Open your windows!) The final glaze should coat the back of a spoon like a thick syrup. Season to taste with salt and pepper.

5) To serve, drizzle the glaze directly over the vegetables in the baking dish, or divide among individual plates and drizzle with about 4 teaspoons of the glaze per serving.

~ Yield: 4 to 6 servings ~

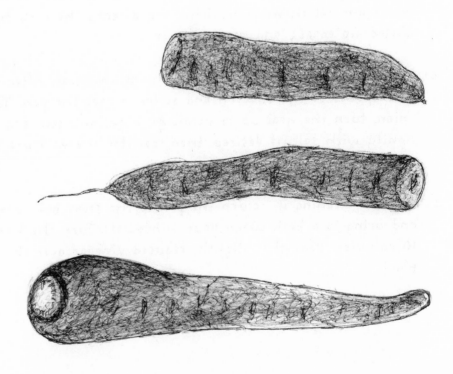

Ruby Chard
Decorated with Itself

We normally think of the leaves as the edible part of this plant, but ruby chard's deep red stems cook up as a tender, delicious little vegetable all on their own. This recipe celebrates it all! You remove the stems from the leaves and cook everything separately (enabling the stems to retain their glorious color), then recombine all the components for a visually stunning side dish.

NOTE:
♥ Chard can carry a lot of silt — and then retain a lot of water on the wavy surfaces of its leaves. So wash and dry it thoroughly before you begin.

1 pound ruby chard, washed in several changes of water and
    thoroughly dried
2 tablespoons extra-virgin olive oil
1 cup minced red onion
Salt, to taste (optional)
⅓ cup balsamic vinegar
Freshly ground black pepper, to taste
½ cup lightly toasted pine nuts (optional)

1) Use a very sharp knife to remove the stems from the chard leaves. Coarsely chop the leaves and set them aside. Trim and discard the very tips of the stems (as well as any dinged-up edges), and mince the rest.

2) Place a medium-sized skillet over medium heat. After about a minute, add about 2 teaspoons of the olive oil and swirl to coat the pan. Toss in the chard stems and the onion, turn the heat up to medium-high, and stir-fry for about 5 minutes. Sprinkle lightly with salt, if desired, then transfer the mixture to a medium-sized bowl, and set aside.

3) Without cleaning it, return the pan to the stove over medium heat. Pour in the vinegar and bring to a boil. (Open your windows!) Turn the heat to very low and simmer for 10 minutes. Pour this slightly reduced vinegar over the stem-onion mixture in the bowl.

4) Return the still uncleaned pan to the stove over medium heat, and wait another minute. Add the remaining olive oil and swirl to coat the pan. Turn up the heat to medium-high and toss in the chard leaves. Cook quickly, turning with tongs as you go, until the leaves are wilted. This will only take a couple of minutes. You can salt the leaves lightly while they cook, if you wish.

5) When the leaves are done to your liking, transfer them to a serving plate or bowl and taste to adjust the salt. Add black pepper to taste, then spoon the stem mixture over the top, being sure to include all the juices. Serve hot, warm, or at room temperature, topped with pine nuts, if desired.

~ Yield: 4 to 6 servings ~

Deep-Flavor SHIITAKE SLAW

Don't be deterred by the long list of ingredients! This recipe is mostly a throw-together-and-let-marinate affair. Delicious as a side dish or an appetizer, this also works beautifully as a relish topping for any grilled fish, tofu, tempeh, or chicken.

NOTE:
♥ The first step needs to be started about an hour in advance (longer is okay), and, once assembled, the slaw needs at least 2 hours to marinate.

1 ounce dried shiitake mushrooms
1 cup finely shredded cabbage
1 medium carrot, shredded
1/4 cup minced red bell pepper
1 scallion, very finely minced
1/8 teaspoon salt
1/2 teaspoon (scant measure) minced or crushed garlic
2 teaspoons light-colored honey
1/2 teaspoon soy sauce
2 tablespoons roasted peanut or walnut oil
1 tablespoon Chinese-style dark sesame oil
1 teaspoon fresh lemon juice
1 small bunch watercress, minced

OPTIONAL TOPPINGS:
♥ Minced or torn cilantro leaves
♥ Minced peanuts or cashews, lightly toasted
♥ Minced crystallized ginger
♥ Chili oil or red pepper flakes

1) Place the shiitakes in a medium-small bowl and pour about 2 cups boiling water over them. Cover the bowl with a plate and let it sit for at least 30 minutes (and for as long as overnight). Drain the mushrooms thoroughly, squeezing out and saving all the liquid for another use, such as soup stock. Remove and discard the stems, then thinly slice the caps and transfer to a medium-large bowl.

2) Add the cabbage, carrot, bell pepper, scallion, and salt, and toss together gently.

3) In a small bowl, whisk together the garlic, honey, soy sauce, oils, and lemon juice until smooth. Pour this into the slaw, stirring to distribute. Cover the bowl and let it sit for at least 2 hours to marinate. (If you're going to let it sit longer, refrigerate it.)

4) Toss in the watercress just before serving, mixing with a fork until uniformly combined. Serve cold or at room temperature, with any or all of the optional toppings.

~ Yield: 4 to 6 servings ~

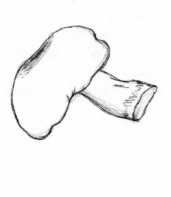

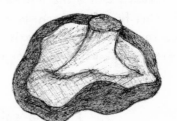

Spinach Bundles
with
Creamy Miso Sauce

Inspired by the Japanese dish Ohitashi, which is served cold as an appetizer, these spinach bundles make a lovely side dish that goes well with grilled fish or tofu.

NOTES:
- ♥ You can find miso (fermented soybean paste) in Asian grocery stores or natural food stores. Ditto the optional bonito flakes. Both of these items will keep on your shelf indefinitely.
- ♥ The honey will blend into the sauce best if warmed a little bit first in a microwave.
- ♥ If using frozen spinach, look for whole leaf rather than chopped—it will work better for this recipe.
- ♥ You can prepare the spinach and the sauce up to several days ahead of time.
- ♥ Store the spinach and sauce in separate, tightly covered containers in the refrigerator, and assemble the dish shortly before serving.

1 pound spinach (fresh or frozen)
¼ cup light-colored miso, such as white or shiro
½ cup cider vinegar
2 tablespoons light-colored honey
¼ teaspoon minced or crushed garlic (optional)
2 tablespoons roasted peanut oil (or almond or sesame)
⅓ cup mayonnaise (or more, to taste)
Red pepper flakes, to taste
A few toasted sesame seeds
Dried bonito flakes (optional)

1) Place the spinach in a colander and rinse well. Shake to remove most, but not all, of the water. (If using frozen spinach, you won't need to cook it. Just let it thaw in a colander by running it under room-temperature tap water and then drain it well, pressing out most of the excess liquid with the back of a spoon. Proceed to step 2, but then skip steps 3 and 4.)

2) Place the miso in a medium-sized bowl. Whisk in the vinegar, honey, optional garlic, oil, and mayonnaise, and beat until smooth. Add a few red pepper flakes to taste, if desired, and adjust the mayonnaise to taste as well. Set aside.

3) Without adding any liquid beyond the water still clinging to the leaves, cook the fresh spinach in any kind of pot over medium-high heat for about a minute, or until thoroughly wilted. Watch it carefully, and turn with tongs while it is cooking, so it doesn't burn.

4) Remove from the heat, and transfer the spinach to a colander in a sink. Let it cool until comfortable to handle, pressing out any excess liquid with the back of a spoon as it cools.

5) Divide the spinach into 4 sections. Use your hands to squeeze out and discard as much of the remaining liquid as possible, then press each section into a tight little bundle of any shape.

6) Spoon the sauce onto 4 or 5 small plates, and place a spinach bundle on top of, or next to, each puddle of sauce. Top the spinach with a light sprinkling of sesame seeds and dried bonito flakes, if available, and serve cold or at room temperature.

~ Yield: 4 servings ~

Creamed Spinach
with Mushrooms

A great omelet filling, this can also multitask as a side dish or a thick sauce/topping for just about any savory dish. Try it on a baked potato.

NOTES:
- ♥ It's easiest to warm the milk directly in its measuring cup in a microwave.
- ♥ This dish keeps for up to a week if stored in a tightly covered container in the refrigerator. You can easily reheat individual servings in a microwave.

> 1 pound fresh baby spinach leaves (or 1 pound frozen chopped spinach)
> 2 to 3 tablespoons canola oil or unsalted butter
> 1/4 teaspoon dry mustard
> 1/8 teaspoon grated nutmeg (possibly more)
> 1/2 pound mushrooms, cleaned, stemmed, and minced
> 3/4 teaspoon salt
> 1 1/2 teaspoons minced or crushed garlic
> 1/4 cup unbleached all-purpose flour
> 2 cups hot milk (any kind)
> White pepper, to taste

1) Place the spinach in a colander and rinse well. Shake to remove most, but not all, of the water clinging to the leaves. (If using frozen spinach, thaw in a colander under running tap water and then let it drain well—pressing out most of the excess liquid with the back of a spoon. It doesn't have to be bone dry—just not soupy.)

2) Heat the oil or melt the butter in a 10-inch sauté pan over low heat. Add the mustard and nutmeg as it melts, then add the mushrooms and 1/4 teaspoon of the salt. Sauté over medium heat for 8 to 10 minutes or until the mushrooms seem cooked through and are beginning to express some liquid. Stir in the garlic.

3) Use a tea strainer to slowly sift in the flour with one hand while you whisk the sautéed mushrooms with the other. Keep whisking for a minute or so after all the flour is in. This will become very thick.

4) Slowly pour in the hot milk, still whisking. As the milk is incorporated, it will become a medium-thick sauce. Keep whisking to keep it smooth.

5) Add the spinach all at once. Use a fork to spread it out, stirring it in as you go. It will take a minute or so to distribute the spinach evenly throughout the sauce. Once it's spread out, sprinkle in the remaining salt.

6) Cook for about 2 more minutes over low heat, stirring frequently with a wooden spoon. Remove the pan from the heat and add white pepper to taste. Serve hot or warm.

~ Yield: 4 to 6 servings, enough to fill 6 omelets ~

GREEK-STYLE SPINACH
w/ Caramelized Onions, Tomatoes, Yogurt, & Pine Nuts

Well-done (and thus very sweet) onions combine beautifully with barely cooked spinach and tomatoes. The yogurt and pine nuts added just before serving make this an exceptionally fresh-tasting dish.

NOTES:
- ♥ You can cook the onions well ahead of time and leave them in the pan on the stove for up to several hours. Reheat the onions, and finish the dish shortly before serving.
- ♥ Use only fresh spinach for this dish! Frozen spinach won't work.
- ♥ You can use chopped fresh tomato or Oven-Scorched "Stewed" Tomatoes (page 120), which, of course, would need to have been made well ahead.

1 pound fresh spinach
2 tablespoons olive oil
1½ cups minced onion
Salt, to taste
1 teaspoon minced or crushed garlic
4 ounces chopped fresh tomatoes
    (or ½ cup chopped Oven-Scorched "Stewed" Tomatoes — page 120)

FOR THE TOP:
- ♥ Plain yogurt (regular or Greek style)
- ♥ Lightly toasted pine nuts
- ♥ Freshly ground black pepper, to taste

1) Stem the spinach, and wash the leaves. Drain (okay to leave a little water clinging to the leaves) and transfer to a cutting board. Coarsely chop and set aside.

2) Place a large, deep skillet or wok over medium heat. After about a minute, add the oil, and swirl to coat the pan. Add the onion, and cook for about 5 minutes, stirring often. Sprinkle lightly with salt, reduce the heat to low, and continue to cook, stirring occasionally, for about 10 minutes longer, or until very soft and sweet.

3) Turn the heat back up to medium, and add the spinach and the garlic to the onion, sprinkling a little salt over the leaves. Use tongs to lift and stir the spinach as it cooks for about 5 minutes, or until just wilted and bright green.

4) Toss in the chopped tomatoes, and cook for just a few minutes longer, still turning with the tongs—until the tomato pieces are heated through.

5) Serve immediately, topping each serving with a dollop of yogurt, a light sprinkling of pine nuts, and a few grinds of black pepper.

~ Yield: 4 to 5 servings ~

1-Minute Spinach

It's very easy to just pop open a package of prewashed baby spinach and dump it into a pan (or bowl, if you are using the microwave). One minute later, you will have a delicious and nutritious vegetable side dish. It will be even more delicious if you use flavorful vegetable broth, such as Imagine brand, and dress the final product with a very fruity olive oil or an aromatic roasted nut or seed oil.

NOTE:
♥ This will keep for up to 5 days in a tightly covered container in the refrigerator.

> 1 pound fresh baby spinach leaves (or 1 pound frozen
>   chopped spinach)
> 3 to 4 tablespoons vegetable broth or water
> Salt, to taste
> A touch of minced or crushed garlic
> Extra-virgin olive oil or a roasted nut or seed oil (optional)

1) Place the spinach in a colander and rinse well. Shake to remove most, but not all, of the water clinging to the leaves. If using frozen spinach, thaw in a colander under running tap water and then let it drain well, pressing out most of the excess liquid with the back of a spoon. (It doesn't have to be bone dry, just not soupy.)

2) Place the broth or water in a medium-sized microwave-safe bowl (if using a microwave) or pot (if using the stove). Cover the bowl with a plate (or the pot with a lid).

3) Microwave the bowl on high power for 1 minute or cook the spinach in the pot over medium-high heat for 1 minute.

4) Remove from the heat, and season to taste with a little salt and a touch of garlic. Finish with a drizzle of flavorful oil, if desired, and serve hot, warm, or at room temperature.

~ Yield: 3 to 4 servings ~

Apple~Maple Broiled Acorn Squash

Simple and sweet with a broiled top, these golden circles will literally round out your dinner plate.

NOTES:

♥ Be careful slicing the squash. Use a very sharp paring knife, inserting the point first and using a gently sawing motion. The easiest way to remove the seeds is to cut loose the strands around them with scissors, and then scrape them away with a spoon.

♥ A high-grade maple syrup (one with very subtle flavor) works best for this.

> Extra-virgin olive oil as needed
> 2 acorn squash (about 1½ pounds each), skin on,
>   and cut into ½-inch rings
> 3 tablespoons defrosted apple juice concentrate
> 1 tablespoon real maple syrup
> Squeezable lemon wedges, for garnish

1) Preheat the oven to 375°F. Line a baking tray with foil and coat it with olive oil. Arrange the squash rings on the prepared tray, brushing their top surface with a little more olive oil.

2) Place the tray in the center of the oven and roast for 10 to 15 minutes, or until the squash is fork-tender. Remove the tray from the oven.

3) In a small bowl, combine the apple juice concentrate and maple syrup. Generously brush this mixture over the top surfaces of the squash rings.

4) Preheat the broiler and move the oven rack to the highest position. Place the tray under the broiler for just a minute or two, until the top begins to brown. (Watch carefully—it can burn quickly.) Remove the tray from the broiler and, if desired, glaze with a touch more of the apple-maple mixture. Serve hot, warm, or at room temperature, with a squeezable lemon wedge alongside.

~ Yield: 4 to 5 servings ~

Spaghetti Squash
WITH Caramelized Onions
AND Crispy Sage Leaves

The flavor of spaghetti squash is subtle, and this multiple baking process deepens it into a delicate sweetness. Consider making a double batch — it doesn't take much more work to do so.

2 to 3 tablespoons extra-virgin olive oil, plus extra for baking
1 (3-pound) spaghetti squash
1 teaspoon unsalted butter (optional)
1½ cups minced onion
1 teaspoon minced or crushed garlic
½ teaspoon salt
Freshly ground black pepper, to taste
Crispy Sage Leaves (follows)

1) Preheat the oven to 425°F. Line a baking tray with foil and coat lightly with olive oil.

2) Cut the squash in half lengthwise and remove the seeds, either by scraping with a spoon or cutting them out with scissors (or both). Place the squash halves, cut-side down, on the tray and bake in the center of the oven for 35 to 40 minutes, or until soft enough to be fairly easily pierced with a fork. Remove the tray from the oven and turn the oven down to 375°F.

3) When the squash is cool enough to handle, scrape it with a fork to let steam escape, separating the cooked strands. Finish scooping with a soup spoon and rake through the strands once again with a fork. There will be about 5 to 6 cups of strands.

4) Add a bit more olive oil to the foil-lined tray and spread it around. Arrange the squash strands on the tray in an even layer and return to the oven for 15 minutes.

5) Meanwhile, place a large skillet over medium heat. After about a minute, add the olive oil and swirl to coat the pan. Melt in the butter, if desired (extra flavor!), then add the minced onion. Sauté over medium heat until softened, about 5 minutes. Add the garlic and salt, and continue cooking and stirring for about 3 minutes, or until the onion is very soft and starting to turn golden.

6) Add the onion mixture to the squash on the tray, mixing everything together as well as you can with a large fork. Return the tray to the oven one more time, turn the oven down to 350°F, and bake, stirring occasionally, for about 30 minutes, or until everything turns a deep golden brown. Serve hot, warm, or at room temperature, topped with ground pepper and a few Crispy Sage Leaves.

~ Yield: 3 to 4 servings ~

Crispy Sage Leaves

I learned this trick in Tuscany, and it was worth the price of several plane tickets! Use these to garnish anything and everything—or just eat them as a snack. They keep beautifully in a jar at room temperature for a week or longer.

NOTES:
- ♥ You must pay very close attention for just a few seconds. (If you try to do this and anything else at the same time, you'll burn the leaves!)
- ♥ Try cooking the first leaf or two separately until you see how fast they go. Different stoves and pans make this an imprecise art.
- ♥ After your great success with sage leaves, try experimenting with other herbs. This also works beautifully with cilantro, parsley, arugula, and basil.

> 1 tablespoon extra-virgin olive oil (or as needed)
> 16 to 20 large, fresh sage leaves, washed and carefully patted dry

1) Line a plate with several layers of paper towels and set aside.

2) Place a small skillet over medium heat. After about a minute, add 1 to 2 teaspoons olive oil—enough to generously coat the bottom of the pan.

3) Add 3 to 4 sage leaves (however many will fit), gently pressing them flat with a fork or the back of a spoon. Cook them for only 5 to 7 seconds, then use tongs or the edge of a pancake turner to carefully flip them over.

4) Cook for about 5 seconds on the other side, or until they turn bright green, with no hint of browning. Quickly transfer the leaves to the prepared plate to drain. They will crispen as they cool.

5) Repeat with the remaining leaves, adding more oil to the pan as needed. Note: If the leaves begin to brown too quickly after your first or second batch, turn the heat down to medium-low.

~ Yield: 4 servings (4 to 5 leaves apiece) ~

Roasted Acorn Squash
with Orange-Cranberry Glaze

Make the delicious glaze while the squash is in the oven, and all will be ready when you are.

NOTE:
♥ The glaze will thicken greatly if you make it well ahead of time. If this is the case, just thin it back to the original consistency with a little water or some extra orange juice and reheat gently.

Extra-virgin olive oil as needed
2 acorn squash (about 1½ pounds each), seeded and cut into quarters
Salt and freshly ground black pepper, to taste
1½ teaspoons cornstarch
½ cup freshly squeezed orange juice (strained to remove pips and pulp)
1 teaspoon finely minced orange zest
1 teaspoon cider vinegar
1½ teaspoons light-colored honey
1½ tablespoons dried cranberries

1) Preheat the oven to 425°F. Line a baking tray with foil and brush with a little olive oil. Brush the cut surfaces of the squash with olive oil as well, and sprinkle lightly with salt and pepper. Arrange the squash, one cut-side down, on the tray and roast for 15 minutes. Turn the squash so the other cut side is now facedown and roast for about 15 minutes longer, or until fork-tender. Remove the tray from the oven and set aside.

2) In a small saucepan, combine the cornstarch with 2 tablespoons of the orange juice and whisk until smooth. Add the remaining orange juice, along with the zest, vinegar, and honey; whisk to combine. Place over medium heat and cook, whisking, for about 5 minutes, or until thick and shiny. (The mixture will turn from milky orange to a translucent glaze.) Remove from the heat and stir in the cranberries. Season to taste with salt and black pepper, if desired.

3) To serve, arrange the squash wedges on a pretty serving platter and drizzle with the glaze—about 2 tablespoons per piece.

~ Yield: 4 servings ~

Roasted Butternut Squash
WITH Roasted Walnut Oil
AND Pomegranate Seeds

The sweetness of a butternut varies greatly from one squash to another. The intensity of its golden color can be, but isn't necessarily, an indicator. So after you roast the squash, give it a taste. If it's plenty sweet, just toss it with the walnut oil and salt—and top with the pomegranate seeds—and you're there. But if it still tastes pale after the walnut oil and salt are in there, proceed with the lime juice-maple syrup treatment, and even the most retrograde squash will shine.

NOTE:
♥ A high-grade maple syrup (one with very subtle flavor) works best for this.

> Nonstick cooking spray for the baking tray
> A 2-pound butternut squash
> 1 tablespoon roasted walnut oil
> 1/8 teaspoon salt
> 1 tablespoon fresh lemon juice or lime juice (optional)
> Up to 1 tablespoon real maple syrup, to taste (optional)
> Seeds from 1 large pomegranate

1) Preheat the oven to 425°F. Line a baking tray with foil and spray generously with nonstick spray.

2) Peel the squash, then slice it in half lengthwise. Use kitchen scissors to loosen the seeds, then scrape them out with a spoon and discard them. Cut the peeled squash into small (1/2- to 3/4-inch) chunks (you'll have about 5 cups of them) and spread them in a single layer on the tray.

3) Bake in the center of the oven for 8 to 10 minutes, or until fork-tender. Try not to let them get mushy.

4) Transfer to a medium-sized bowl, and toss with the walnut oil and some salt. Taste to see if it needs to be enhanced with lemon or lime juice and maple syrup.

5) Serve hot, warm, or at room temperature, topped with pomegranate seeds.

~ Yield: 3 to 4 servings ~

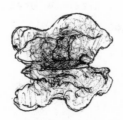

SPAGHETTI SQUASH PANCAKES

Tender, eggy, delicate, soft, and slightly chewy, these pancakes have such a mysterious quality that people will have difficulty guessing what they're made from. In addition to being great for breakfast, they also work well as a side dish or a light entrée for lunch or dinner.

NOTES:
- ♥ Prepare the spaghetti squash well ahead of time. (The instructions follow the recipe.)
- ♥ The batter keeps well for up to 5 days if stored in a tightly covered container in the refrigerator.
- ♥ To keep the pancakes warm, transfer them to a rack on a baking tray, and place the tray in a 200°F oven until serving time. (The rack keeps them crisp.)

> 2 cups cooked spaghetti squash (instructions on opposite page)
> 1 cup minced onion
> ¼ cup unbleached all-purpose flour or rice flour
> ½ teaspoon salt (scant measure)
> 4 large eggs
> Nonstick spray for the pan
> A little unsalted butter for the pan (optional)
>
> OPTIONAL TOPPINGS
> - ♥ Sour cream or yogurt
> - ♥ Minced parsley
> - ♥ Tomato-Basil Jam (page 121)
> - ♥ Caramelized Onion-Orange Marmalade (page 77)

1) Place the cooked squash in a medium-sized bowl and separate the strands by combing through them with a fork. Continue to use the fork to mix in the onion, flour, and salt, and then to beat in the eggs.

2) Place a skillet or griddle over medium heat. After a minute or two, spray it lightly with nonstick spray, and, if you like, melt in a little butter for a richer flavor. When the cooking surface is hot enough to sizzle a bread crumb, use a ¼-cup measure with a handle to scoop batter into the hot pan.

3) Cook the pancakes for a good 8 to 10 minutes on each side—until truly golden. (Unlike cakier pancakes, which toughen when turned repeatedly from side to side, these can be turned more than once, if necessary, without compromising their texture.) Get them really well-done on the outside, and you will have an exquisite chewy-crisp result. Serve hot or warm—plain, or topped with any of the optional toppings.

~ Yield: 4 servings ~

To prepare spaghetti squash for this recipe:

1 (3-pound) spaghetti squash

1) Preheat the oven to 350°F. Cut the squash in half lengthwise, and scrape out the seeds.

2) Bake the halves facedown on a lightly oiled tray for about 30 minutes, or until the skin can be just barely pierced with a fork. (It should be tender, but not too soft.)

3) Remove from the oven, and cool to room temperature. Scoop out the flesh, place it in a strainer, and squeeze out enough of the juices to reduce its final volume to 2 packed cups.

SIMPLEST SUMMER SQUASH

You can make this with any thin-skinned, quick-cooking squash: yellow, summer squash, pattypan, zucchini, crookneck, etc. A combination is nice, especially with varied colors.

NOTE:
♥ This can be expanded into more of a light vegetarian main dish if served over brown rice or barley (or a combination) and topped with the optional pine nuts and cheese.

    1½ to 2 tablespoons extra-virgin olive oil
    2 medium onions, thinly sliced
    ⅛ teaspoon salt (possibly more)
    1½ pounds summer squash (peeling optional), cut into ½-inch-thick
       slices or cubes
    1 teaspoon minced or crushed garlic
    Freshly ground black pepper, to taste

    OPTIONAL TOPPINGS:
    ♥ Minced fresh thyme
    ♥ Lightly toasted pine nuts
    ♥ Crumbed feta or goat cheese

1) Place a large skillet over medium heat. After about a minute, add 1 tablespoon of the olive oil and swirl to coat the pan. Add the onions and salt. Cook, stirring often, for about 10 minutes, or until the onions become very tender and lightly golden. Transfer the onions to a bowl and set them aside.

2) Without cleaning the pan, return it to medium heat, and coat it with a little more olive oil. Add the squash in a single layer and cook without stirring, until very golden on the bottom, 1 to 2 minutes.

3) Scrape the squash loose, and toss or stir to flip it over. Continue cooking, undisturbed, for 1 to 2 minutes longer, or until deeply golden brown on the other side.

4) Toss in the garlic and cook for a minute or so, then return the onions to the pan. Mix well and season to taste with additional salt, if needed, and a good amount of freshly ground black pepper. Serve hot, warm, or at room temperature, garnished with a light sprinkling of thyme, pine nuts, and/or cheese, if desired.

~ Yield: 4 servings ~

SWEET POTATO HASH
with Smoked Tofu and Red Onions

NOTES:

♥ Cook the sweet potatoes ahead of time by boiling or steaming them in their skins. After they cool down, they'll be very easy to peel.

♥ Smoked tofu comes in shrink-wrapped packages, similar to the variously seasoned "savory baked" tofu in the health food section of most grocery stores. If you can't find it, you can also use any soy-based "veggie bacon"-type product in its place.

1 to 2 tablespoons extra-virgin olive oil
2 cups minced red onion
2½ pounds sweet potatoes—cooked, peeled, and diced
2 teaspoons minced or crushed garlic
½ teaspoon salt (or to taste)
Freshly ground black pepper, to taste
About 4 ounces smoked tofu, cut into thin strips
Balsamic vinegar (regular, or the reduced, thickened kind)
Hard-boiled eggs, cut into wedges (optional)

1) Place a large skillet over medium heat. After about a minute, add 1 tablespoon of the olive oil and swirl to coat the pan. Add the onions and sauté for about 5 to 8 minutes, or until the onions are soft and translucent.

2) Add a little more olive oil to the pan, then stir in the sweet potatoes, garlic, and salt, spreading the mixture out to allow maximum contact with the hot pan. Wait about 5 minutes, then stir it around again, letting it cook until everything becomes exquisitely crisp.

3) Season to taste with black pepper, then stir in the tofu. Taste to adjust the salt and serve hot, drizzled with balsamic vinegar (or balsamic reduction) and garnished with wedges of hard-boiled egg, if desired.

~ Yield: 4 to 5 servings ~

oven~"fried" Sweet Potatoes

NOTES:

♥ Sweet potatoes acquire a chewy, spunky texture when "fried" in the oven. This is even more pronounced if you leave them in at a low temperature to dry out and crispen up after the initial baking.

♥ I prefer high-oleic safflower oil for this dish. It has a high smoke point, which helps prevent burning and creates a spunkier texture.

♥ The finished texture has much to do with the size and shape of the pieces. Thinner batons will yield a chewier, crisper result.

> 3 tablespoons high-oleic safflower oil or extra-virgin olive oil
> 2 pounds sweet potatoes
> Salt, to taste

1) Preheat the oven to 375°F. Line 2 baking trays with foil and coat each with 1½ tablespoons oil.

2) Peel the sweet potatoes and use a very sharp knife to cut them first into thin slices (¼ inch or less) and then into long batons at ¼-inch intervals. (These measures are all approximate, of course.)

3) Arrange the batons in single layers on the baking trays and place the trays in the oven. After 10 minutes, use tongs to turn the sweet potatoes over and let them bake another 5 to 10 minutes on the second side until fork-tender. (Careful not to let them burn! This will depend on the thickness of the pieces, so you'll need to watch them.)

4) If you like softer "fries," take them out of the oven now. If you prefer a crisper result, turn the oven down to 200°F and leave the trays in there for up to 20 minutes. (This will give the sweet potatoes a chance to dry out a little and acquire some texture. They will shrink somewhat in volume.) Remove the trays from the oven, salt the sweet potatoes lightly, and serve hot, warm, or at room temperature.

~ Yield: 4 servings ~

Vanilla & Maple Sweet Potatoes

Subtle.

....

NOTE:
- ♥ A high-grade maple syrup (one with very subtle flavor) works best for this.

     5 pounds sweet potatoes (about 10 medium-sized ones)
     3/4 teaspoon salt
     1 tablespoon plus 1 teaspoon vanilla extract
     2 tablespoons real maple syrup
     1 teaspoon fresh lemon or lime juice
     Nonstick cooking spray (optional, if reheating)

....

1) Peel the sweet potatoes and cut into chunks. Cook in boiling water until soft (about 15 to 20 minutes). Drain well and transfer to a large bowl.

2) Add the salt, vanilla, maple syrup, and lemon or lime juice, and stir and mash until smooth. (A handheld electric mixer at medium speed does this very well.)

3) Serve right away or let stand at room temperature (or in the refrigerator, covered tightly) until serving time.

4) To reheat, preheat the oven to 350°F and spray a 9 x 13-inch baking pan with nonstick spray. Spread the sweet potato mixture evenly into place, cover tightly with foil, and place in the center of the oven for as long as needed to come to the desired temperature. (The length of the reheating time depends on how cold the sweet potatoes were to begin with. Just keep checking as they reheat.)

....

~ Yield: 6 or more servings ~

ROASTED TARRAGON SUCCOTASH

A new twist on the classic corn and lima bean combo. It requires only a few minutes of your effort, then bakes into a fabulous dish all by itself with no further help from you. The fresh tarragon infuses your kitchen as well as the dish!

NOTES:
- ♥ If you have access to fresh sweet corn and you feel like shaving it off the cobs, go ahead and substitute this for the frozen. You will need about 6 ears of corn.
- ♥ This doesn't have to be made with lima beans. Try using frozen green soybeans (edamame) or, if you can find them, frozen green chickpeas (really special!).

> 2 to 3 tablespoons extra-virgin olive oil
> 1 (1-pound) package frozen lima beans (or lima bean option)
> 1 (1-pound) package frozen corn
> 1 bulb garlic, cloves peeled and halved lengthwise
> 1 small bunch fresh tarragon (about a handful), coarsely chopped
> 1 heaping cup olives, pitted and sliced (optional)
> Salt and freshly ground black pepper, to taste
> 2 tablespoons balsamic vinegar (optional)

1) Preheat the oven to 375°F. Line a large baking tray with foil and coat with olive oil.

2) Place the beans, corn, and garlic cloves on the tray, and toss on the tarragon and olives, if using. Shake the tray around a bit to combine and distribute everything, then spread out the ingredients into a single layer and cover tightly with foil.

3) Bake for 50 minutes, or until the beans are tender when pierced with a toothpick or a fork. Transfer to a bowl, and add salt and pepper to taste. For added sparkle, you can drizzle in the vinegar. Serve hot, warm, or at room temperature.

~ Yield: 6 servings ~

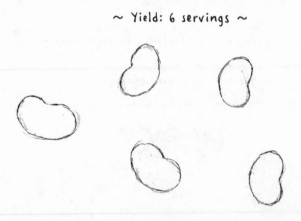

Gratinéed Tomatoes

Thick slices of tomato are seasoned with herbs and sautéed until crispy on the outside, and warm and soft within.

NOTES:
- ♥ This works best if served warm, rather than piping hot. The insides of the tomatoes become hotter than the coating, so if you don't let them cool down a little, the hot tomato juices could burn your mouth.
- ♥ The optional butter goes a long way for flavor.

> 4 medium-sized firm tomatoes
> ⅓ cup unbleached all-purpose flour
> 3 tablespoons cornmeal
> 1 tablespoon dried basil
> 2 teaspoons dried tarragon
> 1 teaspoon dried thyme
> Salt, to taste
> Freshly ground black pepper, to taste
> 1 to 2 tablespoons extra-virgin olive oil
> About 1 teaspoon unsalted butter (optional)
> ¼ cup grated Parmesan or fontina cheese (optional)

1) Core the tomatoes and slice them laterally into thick rounds (½ inch or more).

2) On a large plate, combine the flour, cornmeal, and dried herbs with a big pinch of salt and some black pepper. Stir until well blended, then dredge the tomato slices in this mixture, pushing as much of the dry mixture as you can into the crevices of the tomatoes.

3) Place a large, deep skillet over medium heat. After about a minute, add 1 tablespoon of the olive oil and swirl to coat the pan. If you like, you can also melt in some butter.

4) Add the tomatoes to the pan, sautéing on each side for about 10 minutes, or until crisp and lightly browned. Transfer to a large plate and wait about 5 to 10 minutes to serve.

5) If you wish to add the cheese, preheat the broiler and use another tablespoon of olive oil to coat a baking pan or gratin dish. Arrange the tomatoes close together (touching is okay) in the prepared pan or dish. Sprinkle lightly with cheese and broil for just a few minutes, or until golden. Cool for about 10 minutes before serving.

~ Yield: 4 to 5 servings ~

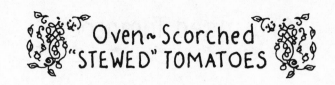

Oven~Scorched "STEWED" TOMATOES

A high-temperature treatment creates its own kind of seasoning, and is so effective on tomatoes they need nothing else — not even salt and pepper, unless someone insists on these at the table.

NOTES:
- ♥ You don't need to peel the tomatoes for this recipe. The skins become part of the texture of the dish.
- ♥ This dish keeps for up to two weeks if tightly covered and refrigerated.

        2 tablespoons extra-virgin olive oil
        5 pounds ripe-but-firm tomatoes

1) Preheat the oven to 425°F. Line a baking tray with foil and coat it with the olive oil.

2) Cut the tomatoes in half; squeeze out and discard the seeds. Place the tomatoes cut-side up on the prepared tray. Place the tray in the center of the oven for 30 minutes. (While they are roasting, visit the tomatoes once or twice with a baster, tilting the tray and siphoning off the juices that the tomatoes emit as they cook. You can save this liquid for soup stock or for cooking rice.)

3) After 30 minutes, remove the tray from the oven and heat the broiler. Place the oven rack at the closest position to the heat and put the tray back in so the tomatoes can broil. Leave them there for about 5 minutes or until the tops are compellingly singed (judgment call on your part).

4) Remove the tray from the oven and transfer the tomatoes to a serving bowl, scraping in whatever you can (and deem edible) of the parts that may have stuck to the foil. Cover the bowl with a plate and let it sit for at least 5 minutes before serving. Serve hot, warm, or at room temperature.

~ Yield: 4 to 5 servings ~

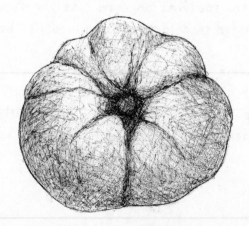

TOMATO-BASIL JAM

Tomato-Basil Jam fits well in any context where you might serve tomato ketchup—it's more complex, yet basically similar. I like this with potatoes, or on top of just about any cornmeal- or polenta-based dish. It's also perfect with Spaghetti Squash Pancakes (page 112).

NOTES:
♥ You can make this with tomatoes of any color or degree of ripeness. Ripe tomatoes will give you a sweeter jam; hard ones will produce a delightfully tart result. I like it both ways.
♥ To peel and seed a tomato, plunge it into simmering water for a slow count of 10 (for a ripe tomato) or 20 (if the tomato is only medium-ripe). Remove the tomato from the water, and pull off the skin. Then cut the tomato in half, and squeeze out and discard the seeds. (You only need to do this with ripe or medium-ripe tomatoes. Unripe tomatoes can go in unedited.)
♥ The two different vinegars add layers of flavor.

2 pounds tomatoes (peeled and seeded, if ripe)
¼ teaspoon salt
3 to 4 tablespoons light-colored honey
2 tablespoons balsamic vinegar
2 teaspoons cider vinegar
About 5 sprigs fresh basil

1) Cut the tomatoes into small cubes and place them in a medium-sized saucepan. Cover the pot, and place it over medium heat.

2) When the tomatoes begin to boil, reduce the heat to medium, uncover the pot, and let it cook for 10 minutes. If it seems dry, you can add a splash or two of water.

3) Stir in the remaining ingredients, and continue to let it cook uncovered over medium heat for another 35 minutes, or until it has been reduced to approximately ⅓ its original volume. (This is inexact—just eyeball it.)

4) Remove the pot from the heat, and dig out and discard the basil. Let the mixture cool to room temperature, then transfer to a clean jar with a tight-fitting lid, and store for up to several weeks in the refrigerator.

~ Yield: About 1⅓ cups ~

RICE-FRIED VEGETABLES

In this vegetable-fried rice reversal, the vegetables are dominant and the rice secondary. Hence the name.

NOTES:
- ♥ The leafy green can be kale, collard, spinach, or chard—the freshest and best you can find.
- ♥ This is a great way to use up leftover rice. However, if you need to cook it fresh, begin with 2 cups uncooked long-grain brown rice and make it well ahead of time. It will yield 3 cups cooked rice.

> 1 tablespoon plus 1 teaspoon canola oil or peanut oil
> 2 large eggs, beaten
> 1½ cups chopped onion
> 1 tablespoon minced ginger
> Salt, to taste
> 4 cups chopped broccoli
> ½ to ¾ pound asparagus or green beans
> 1 medium carrot, cut in thin slices on the diagonal
> 1½ to 2 teaspoons garlic
> 4 cups (packed) chopped leafy greens (stemmed, if necessary)
> 1½ cups peas (frozen and defrosted)
> 2 to 3 cups cooked long-grain brown rice
> 1 tablespoon soy sauce
> 2 to 3 scallions, minced
> ⅔ cup lightly toasted almonds, whole or sliced (optional)

1) Place a small skillet over medium heat. After about a minute, add 1 teaspoon of the oil and swirl to coat the pan. Wait another 30 seconds or so, then pour in the beaten eggs. Tilt the pan in all directions to let the eggs flow to the edges, lifting the cooked edges of the eggs to allow the uncooked eggs to flow underneath. (You are making an omelet!) Flip it over for a second, then transfer to a plate and cut into strips.

2) Place a large, deep skillet over medium heat. After about a minute, add the remaining oil and swirl to coat the pan. Add the onion and ginger, and a couple dashes of salt, and sauté for 5 minutes, or until the onion becomes translucent. Stir in the broccoli, asparagus or green beans, carrot, and garlic. Add another dash or two of salt, if desired, and stir-fry over medium heat for 8 to 10 minutes, or until the vegetables are tender-crisp (up to you).

3) Stir in the chopped leafy greens, turning them into the other vegetables with tongs. Cook for just a couple of minutes, until they turn bright green and wilt slightly.

4) Defrost the peas by placing them in a strainer and running them under cool tap water. Drain thoroughly.

5) Use a fork to fluff in the rice, keeping the grains separate as they join the mixture. Sprinkle in the soy sauce, scallions, and omelet strips, and mix gently until well combined. Serve hot, topped with the peas, and some almonds, if desired.

~ Yield: 4 to 6 servings ~

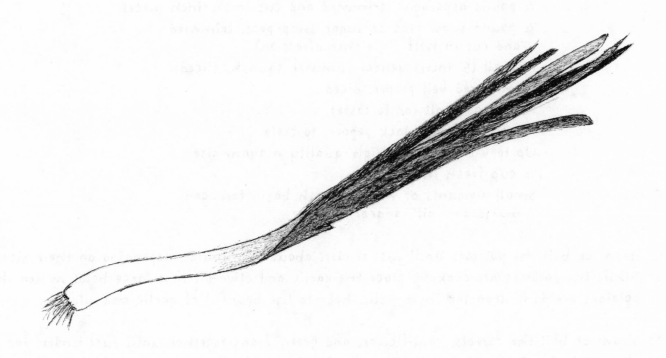

The Best Marinated Vegetables

The ideal vegetables for this salad are the most angelic: miniature squash, baby carrots, slender green beans, flat snow peas, fingerling potatoes, and the like. So use the most innocent-looking vegetables you can find. Also, feel free to make substitutions as necessary. This is a very flexible recipe.

NOTES:
- ♥ The first steps of the recipe have you steaming or boiling the vegetables in groups. With either setup, you can just keep the pot going on the stove and put the vegetables in (and take them out) in shifts.
- ♥ The salad can be assembled a day in advance. Just hold off on adding the lemon juice and fresh herbs until shortly before serving.

8 to 10 fingerling potatoes, halved
1 teaspoon minced or crushed garlic
¼ cup extra-virgin olive oil
¼ pound baby carrots, halved lengthwise
1 small head cauliflower, in 1-inch florets
½ pound fresh green beans, trimmed and cut in half
½ pound asparagus, trimmed and cut in 1½-inch pieces
½ pound snow peas or sugar snap peas, trimmed
    and cut in half (in either direction)
1 small (5-inch) yellow summer squash, sliced
1 small red bell pepper, diced
½ teaspoon salt (or to taste)
Freshly ground black pepper, to taste
Up to 5 tablespoons high-quality mayonnaise
½ cup fresh lemon juice
Small amounts of minced fresh basil, tarragon,
    marjoram, dill, and/or chives

1) Steam or boil the potatoes until just tender, about 10 minutes, depending on their size. While the potatoes are cooking, place the garlic and olive oil in a large bowl. When the potatoes are done, transfer them—still hot—to the bowlful of garlic and oil.

2) Steam or boil the carrots, cauliflower, and green beans together until *just* tender, for about 5 to 8 minutes. Immediately refresh under cold running water, drain well, and transfer to the bowl.

3) Steam or blanch the asparagus, snow peas, and squash until just al dente. (This will take less than 5 minutes.) Immediately refresh under cold running water, drain well, and add to the rest of the vegetables.

4) Add the red pepper, salt, black pepper to taste, and mayonnaise, and stir gently until blended. Cover tightly and let marinate for at least 2 hours at room temperature. (If it's going to sit longer, refrigerate.)

5) Stir in the lemon juice within about 15 minutes of serving time. Taste to correct the salt and pepper, and serve at room temperature or cold, topped with a minced assortment (or just one) of your favorite fresh herbs.

~ Yield: 5 to 6 servings ~

ZUCCHINI·MINT CROQUETTES

leaf leaf leaf leaf leaf leaf leaf leaf leaf

I was very impressed with a fancier version of these delicious little Parmesan-laced puffs made painstakingly by hand (no food processor in sight!) in a cooking class in Tuscany. After the demonstration, the fresh, hot croquettes were served next to a mound of heavenly ricotta cheese on top of a salad, wilting the greens ever so slightly. You can serve these that way if you like, but they are also great as a side dish all by themselves.

My simplified version uses a food processor and takes only minutes to throw together.

NOTE:
♥ Any unused batter will keep for 2 to 3 days in a tightly covered container in the refrigerator. Cooked croquettes will store and reheat well in a hot frying pan or a toaster oven. A microwave will also work, but will undo the crispness.

> 1 cup (packed) fresh mint leaves
> 1 to 2 medium cloves garlic, peeled
> 2 small (4- to 5-ounce) zucchini
> ½ cup fine bread crumbs
> 1 cup grated Parmesan cheese
> 1 large egg, beaten
> Extra-virgin olive oil, as needed

1) Place the mint and garlic in a food processor fitted with the steel blade, and process until fine and feathery.

2) Without emptying or cleaning the food processor, switch to the grating attachment (regular- or medium-sized holes, not tiny) and grate the zucchini into the mint mixture.

3) Transfer to a medium-sized bowl, and add the bread crumbs, Parmesan, and egg. Mix with a fork until thoroughly combined.

4) Place a medium-sized frying pan over medium heat and wait about 2 to 3 minutes. Add a generous amount of olive oil (enough to easily cover the bottom) and swirl to coat the pan. Wait another 30 seconds or so for the oil to become very hot.

5) Add rounded teaspoons of the batter to the hot oil, pressing them down slightly when they hit the pan. (It's easiest to do this with 2 teaspoons, forming little round dumplings between them, as you would make quenelles.) Cook for about 3 minutes on each side, or until deep golden brown.

6) Transfer to a plate lined with a double thickness of paper towels, and leave them there for about a minute before serving them.

~ Yield: About 4 servings ~

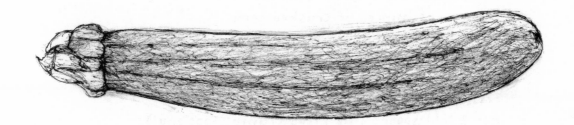

Parmesan-Crusted Zucchini

Tender and moist, with a pungent, crunchy top, these take less than 15 minutes from start to finish.

1 tablespoon extra-virgin olive oil
2 teaspoons minced or crushed garlic
4 small zucchini and/or summer squash
   (slender ones, about 6 inches long), halved lengthwise
Salt, to taste
Freshly ground black pepper, to taste
1 to 2 tablespoons fine bread crumbs (optional)
2 to 3 tablespoons grated Parmesan cheese

1) Preheat the broiler.

2) Place a medium-sized skillet over medium heat. After about a minute, add the olive oil and swirl to coat the pan. Turn down the heat, add the garlic, and sauté over medium-low heat for just a minute or two, being careful not to let the garlic brown.

3) Place the zucchini halves facedown in the garlic butter and sprinkle lightly with salt and pepper. Sauté over medium-high heat for about 5 minutes, or until the zucchini are just slightly tender when poked gently with a fork.

4) Turn the zucchini over and sprinkle generously, first with bread crumbs, if desired, and then with Parmesan. You can also combine the bread crumbs and Parmesan, and sprinkle them on together as a single mixture, if you like. (Note: Don't worry if this topping spills into the pan. It will melt into additional, delicious crust.) Cook for just a minute or two more, then transfer the skillet to the broiler.

5) Broil for about 3 to 5 minutes, or until the cheese is melted and golden brown. Serve hot, and don't forget to scrape up the spilled, now-crispy Parmesan from the bottom of the pan.

~ Yield: 4 to 6 servings ~

TEN WAYS

... to sneak a few more vegetables into your diet ...

Prepare extra vegetables on a regular basis, and use the extras and leftovers in all of these wonderful ways:

1) Vertical Pizza

Pile leftover vegetables (grilled, steamed, marinated)—or simply some fresh green salad onto your favorite thin-crusted pizza.

2) Vegetable Noodles

Here's a great new habit to develop: Add increasing quantities of delicious cooked vegetables to your favorite pasta dish, with any kind of sauce. The goal: a one-to-one ratio of pasta and vegetables—or the vegetables may even edge out the noodles. Season it well with extra-virgin olive oil, herbs, garlic—and a light sprinkling of some flavorful, sharp cheese.

3) Vegetable-Stuffed Potatoes

Hollow out (or mostly hollow out) a baked potato and fill it with a generous amount of sautéed, steamed, or grilled vegetables (freshly prepared or leftover). Top with just the smallest amount of grated cheese and briefly broil.

4) Wraps!

Use a very sharp knife to cut a lot of vegetables (like bell peppers, tomatoes, red onion, cucumber, romaine lettuce, and watercress) into shreds or similarly tiny units. Season lightly with salt and pepper and drizzle with a little extra-virgin olive oil. Anytime you pack a pita sandwich, shoehorn in as much of this vegetable mixture as you can. Roll into a flour tortilla, a pita, or a very thin omelet.

5) Green Eggs (with or without Ham)

Fold leftover vegetables into your scrambled eggs (you don't need to make an official omelet). You can also just scramble some freshly minced broccoli or chopped spinach directly into your eggs. Give the vegetables a little head start in the hot oil or melted butter. When they turn bright green, add the eggs and scramble to your desired taste.

6) The Very Tall Sandwich

Eat your sandwich open-faced, and pile it high with as many vegetables (leftover cooked or freshly chopped/sliced/torn raw) as you can. They will fall off, so eat it over a plate.

7) Almost-Instant Vegetable Soup

Puréeing vegetables into soup is one of the easiest and most delightful ways to go green(er) with your diet. The best vegetables for this purpose are broccoli and spinach, both of which work as well frozen-chopped as fresh-chopped. Use one part broth to one part vegetables (1 cup to 1 cup, or 2 cups to 2 cups, etc.). Heat the broth, add the vegetables, and let it come to a boil. Lower the heat to a simmer and cook for 3 minutes. Let it stand for about 5 minutes, then purée all or part to your liking in a stand-blender or with an immersion blender. There are several good vegetable broths available commercially, my favorite being Imagine brand Organic Vegetable Broth, which is available in most grocery stores, unrefrigerated in 1-quart boxes (similar to soy milk packaging). It will keep for months before being opened. (Once opened, it will last about a week in your refrigerator.)

8) Vegetables, Dressed

Toss any leftover cooked vegetables with your favorite salad dressing for an instant marinated side dish or appetizer that you can serve cold or at room temperature.

9) Vegetables, Dipped

Raw vegetables—baby carrots, celery sticks, bell pepper pieces, peeled broccoli stems, cauliflower florets, very tight, clean, small mushrooms (halved or whole), sugar snap peas, cherry tomatoes, fresh, whole green beans, and more—can all become great snacks when dipped into any delicious substance that will stick. You can make your own dip or use a commercial salsa or salad dressing. Nut butter (any kind), straight from the jar, is terrific for this, and so is commercial spaghetti sauce (a healthy favorite for kids). Use your imagination and chips will become a thing of the past (or a thing for special occasions).

10) Vegetable Juice

If you would like to enhance your vegetable intake but it seems like a chore to actually eat more vegetables, consider investing in a juicer and drinking your vegetables. Homemade juice will give you all the vitamins and nutrients—minus the bulk and fiber—of the vegetables from which it was extracted, enabling you to consume a greater quantity of vegetable goodness than you possibly could otherwise. And vegetable juice is easy to drink in the morning—it goes down really smoothly.

Try a combination of carrot and celery juice in equal parts as a basic blend. To this, you can add smaller amounts of juice from other vegetables, like leafy greens (especially spinach or watercress), bell peppers, fennel, parsley, cabbage, cucumbers, and beets. And if you want to sweeten the mix, add some fresh-pressed apple juice as well—it will soften the edges. (Normally, fruit and vegetable juices don't mix successfully, but apple juice is an exception—it seems to go with everything.)

❧❧ STOCKING YOUR PANTRY ❧❧

se this checklist for stocking your pantry, and delicious vegetable dishes will readily become a natural extension of your day—something you will actually look forward to preparing, serving, and, most important, eating!

♥ Extra-virgin Olive Oil

Some cooks advise using less expensive types of olive oil for cooking and reserving extra-virgin for salad dressings and for "finishing." But I recommend doing what the Italians do: They simply use extra-virgin whenever olive oil is called for. In fact, there is no other designation in Italy and they wouldn't have it any other way! So once you are all set up with your own personally chosen regular brand of everyday extra-virgin, you can go one step further and buy a high-end, extra-fruity, extra-virgin olive oil (one that you've tasted and fallen in love with). Use this for the ultra finishing touch at the table on those special dishes that just cry out for that additional inch.

♥ Canola Oil or Peanut Oil

Some dishes (notably Asian ones) taste better when made with a more neutral flavored oil than olive oil. Canola or plain peanut oil (as opposed to roasted peanut oil, which has a major flavor presence—see below) are good choices for sautéing vegetables when the olive flavor is not a match for the other seasonings.

♥ Roasted Nut and Seed Oils

Roasted almond, walnut, hazelnut, peanut, pumpkin seed, and sesame seed oil are all major sources of deep, toasty flavor when drizzled onto vegetable dishes. (Note that they are seasonings and, with the exception of roasted peanut oil, which has a high smoke point, they should not be used for cooking. They break down at high temperatures.) These exquisite products tend to be expensive but a little bit goes far, and you can keep them in the refrigerator to extend their lifespan. They are also nutritious—an excellent form of healthy monounsaturated fat that we should go out of our way to include in our diet.

~ 131

♥ Nut and Seed Butters

Keep a supply of natural peanut, almond, cashew, and sesame butter (and/or tahini) on hand to use as dips for raw or lightly steamed vegetables, or to thin and season into exotic sauces.

♥ Balsamic Vinegar — Regular or Reduced

This is a great seasoning in its fully liquid form. And the balsamic flavor intensifies as it sits around and slowly evaporates. You can help this along by simply storing it with the top off (a trick I discovered by mistake). Or if you like it thicker with a deeper, sweeter flavor, you can simmer it in a shallow pan over low heat, causing it to reduce. Be careful not to burn it and take it off the stove at any point along the way to 50 percent reduced. At this point, the vinegar will have become a luxurious finishing touch that can be drizzled over vegetables as a topping. Store it indefinitely in a jar at room temperature. (Microwave for just a few seconds to thin it for use, if necessary.)

♥ A Variety of Vinegars

It's nice to keep an assortment on hand — vinegars made from cider, rice wine (both the seasoned and unseasoned kinds), red wine, sherry, and anything else you like and can find on the supermarket shelf.

♥ Onions

Buy small quantities frequently, so they stay fresh and crisp. Store them in a cool, dry, dark place.

♥ Garlic and Fresh Ginger

As with onions, buy both of these frequently so they will be very fresh. Unlike onions, store these in the refrigerator. You can also freeze minced garlic and ginger if you double-wrap them airtight in plastic. Use as desired without defrosting. In the case of fresh ginger, you can also store big pieces of it in a tightly covered jar of white wine or dry sherry in the refrigerator. The wine will preserve the ginger, and the ginger will spike the wine, which will then become a magical elixir for splashing onto your sautéed vegetables!

- ♥ **Vegetable Broth**

This is a great item to have on hand, for all sorts of purposes. As I mentioned earlier, my favorite is Imagine brand, which is available in most grocery stores.

- ♥ **Frozen Vegetables**

Frozen spinach, lima beans, green soybeans, corn, peas, and artichoke hearts are all respectable products that I use often. I even use chopped frozen broccoli sometimes, which is very good for puréeing into quick soups.

- ♥ **Some Nice Salt and a Full Pepper Mill**

I use regular sea salt for cooking but sometimes enjoy putting a fancier, "designer" salt on the table at serving time (in a tiny salt vessel with an even tinier spoon). This is fun and exotic, but not essential. A full pepper mill, on the other hand, is indispensable!

- ♥ **Nuts and Seeds**

I keep an assortment of nuts and seeds in sealed plastic bags in the freezer so they will not become rancid. I take them out as needed, often lightly toasting them in a toaster oven or in a skillet on the stovetop. As you will see in these recipes, lightly toasted nuts and seeds are a frequently used topping in my cooking style!

- ♥ **Bread Crumbs (or Bread at the Ready to Become Crumbs)**

Another frequently used topping! Once in a while, when a recipe calls for very fine crumbs, I will use a commercially prepared kind, for convenience. But when coarse crumbs are appropriate, I prefer to make my own from a high-quality bread. It's an easy and enjoyable little project (and a good outlet for pent-up energy!) and the result will be as good as the bread itself, so choose carefully—you will find that stellar bread becomes equally stellar crumbs. Keep bits and pieces of very good bread stored in your freezer for this purpose.

- ♥ **Hard Grating Cheeses**

A touch here or there of delicious, grated, Italian-style cheese can take vegetable dishes over the top. Freezer storage is best for longer term, mold-free storage, so you can buy a substantial amount and use just a little at a time without worries (or finding weird, fur-coated units in your refrigerator months—or years—hence).

♥ Lemons and Limes

I always have a bowlful on my counter. The hand juicer is right next to it, with a serrated knife and cutting board just inches further. This setup makes a beautiful little still life that you can stare at when you are not cooking and reach for when you are.

♥ Dried Fruit

Similar to nuts, seeds, bread crumbs, and cheese, touches of dried fruit make a wonderful vegetable accessory, in small doses, on more dishes than you might imagine.

♥ Red Pepper Flakes

If you like a little kick of heat and a lovely finished visual effect, then these are for you. If you have access to a good Middle Eastern market, try dried Aleppo pepper, from Syria. It is very beautiful and the flavor is distinctly wonderful.

♥ Cumin

Whole cumin seeds and ground cumin are both in my kitchen at all times. I think I use this seasoning more than any other, except perhaps garlic.

♥ Dried Herbs and Spices

Buy small amounts frequently and throw them out after a month or so. The best way to purchase these is by the ounce at a good ethnic market or out-of-the-way idiosyncratic "gourmet" shop. If you can't find a place that will sell you bulk spices, consider keeping your supply in the freezer, to keep them potent.

♥ Fresh Herbs (Windowsill Garden)

Consider planting some pots with parsley, sage, rosemary, and thyme. And basil, cilantro, and mint. Not only will you be able to snip fresh herbs as needed for crowning touches on many of these recipes, but this will allow you to honestly answer "yes," when asked if you have a garden, even if you live on the twelfth floor. All you need is a sunny window, a watering can, and enthusiasm.

♥ Dijon Mustard and Capers

Always keep them in your refrigerator and use them often.

♥ **Light-Colored Honey and High-Grade, Real Maple Syrup**

With both of these natural sweeteners, the lighter the color, the milder the flavor.

♥ **Soy Sauce**

Use a good, low-sodium variety. My favorite is San-J brand Organic Wheat-Free Reduced Sodium Tamari Soy Sauce.

♥ **Dried Mushrooms**

Keep a supply of dried shiitake and porcini mushrooms on hand. Just half an ounce, soaked and minced (with the flavor-packed soaking water thrown in as well), can powerfully affect the flavor of a dish. Look for bargains on the Internet, and consider buying them in bulk. Keep in mind that dried mushrooms will keep in your cupboard indefinitely.

KITCHEN EQUIPMENT

Vou don't need a high-tech, state-of-the-art kitchen to prepare the very simple vegetable recipes in this book. In fact, you can do every task with just a few key items and come out with beautiful results. But don't skimp on the quality of those few choice tools! Invest in equipment that feels right to you. You will be rewarded in many ways—not the least of which will be your greatly increased happiness in the kitchen and love of the craft that is cooking!

My Six Essentials

♥ An excellent **knife** that feels good in your hand. For many people, a good knife is the determining factor in vegetable preparation. Look for one with a sharp, straight-edged 6- or 8-inch blade, and make sure you love it at first grip. A knife is a very personal tool, so choose it carefully.

♥ **Cutting boards**, wooden or synthetic. These are best if they're portable, so you can move them from counter to stove to sink with ease.

♥ A wide (12-inch or larger diameter) **skillet** with a cover. The best ones are made of heavy-gauge metal with an exterior of either stainless steel or enamel-coated steel (my favorite). Even though my kitchen contains several sets of professional-quality cookware that I've had for decades, I find myself reaching for that one enamel-coated skillet for practically everything. Everyone should have that one great pan! Sometimes it's a trial and error process to get there, but when you've found The One, you'll just know. (You don't need to worry about nonstick surfaces when cooking with good cookware if you get the pan nice and hot ahead of time and use an appropriate amount of healthy oil, such as the ones these recipes provide.)

- A **colander** or two (or three) of various sizes. You'll need to wash and drain many of your ingredients and there is no better tool for this purpose.

- **Spring-loaded tongs.** This is the best vegetable-grabbing device in the world! I need to have these in my hand once I put down the cherished knife and get the pan going.

- A set of good **storage containers** with tight-fitting tops, and a supply of heavy-duty zip-style plastic bags. Many of these recipes can (and in fact, should) be prepared in advance and reheated, and good storage containers make this possible.

Other Useful Tools

- **Food processor** with good, sharp blades and a grating attachment. Your work and meal preparations can be made much shorter if you have one of these on hand.

- **A large wok.** This can be a great backup to your cherished, much-used, above-mentioned skillet. It's fun to do large stir-fries in these big, deep vessels and the heat distribution is stellar.

- **Oven trays** (and foil to line them). The classic unfancy roasting kit. Just add olive oil and vegetables, and head for the preheated oven.

- **Scissors.** I use them constantly for dozens of minor operations, from snipping herbs to trimming artichokes to loosening and removing the seeds from pumpkins and winter squash.

- **Large, deep saucepan.** There is nothing better for blanching vegetables, which means boiling water, lowering the heat to a simmer, and giving the vegetables a quick dunk. You'll find yourself doing this a *lot* in many of these recipes.

- **Salad spinner.** This tool is useful for when you want every last drop of water gone from your freshly washed green leaves.

- **Small hand grater.** For a spot of cheese or a touch of carrot, beet, or red cabbage for garnish. Very handy!

- **Microplane grater.** Magical for citrus zest.

- **Garlic press** (if you prefer crushed over minced). Be sure to choose a heavy-gauge one with a comfortable handle.

- Good, sturdy **vegetable peeler.** Also good for citrus zest.

- **Citrus zester.** You can use the microplane grater to remove the zest from an orange, lime, or lemon, but a bona fide zester is a lot of fun, too.

- **Mandoline.** This is the best tool for shaving paper-thin slices of cucumber, fennel, lemon, and many other things. You don't need to spend a fortune on a high-end one, either. Shop in the ethnic and Asian markets for a small, bargain version, which will work just as well as the heavier ones from the cuisine store. Remember to pay careful attention when using this very sharp gadget! I know many experienced (even professional) cooks who have seriously sliced their knuckles, double-tasking (or even just glancing away) while operating a mandoline.

- **Natural fiber towels** for your hands and/or your freshly washed produce. Paper towels are handy, but soft, cotton ones are more aesthetically appealing and ecological. Keep a clean supply at the ready and your kitchen will feel even homier than it already does.

- **Toaster oven.** This comes in very handy for toasting small amounts of nuts, seeds, or coconut, and sometimes for reheating single portions of gratins and other vegetable dishes.

INDEX